IN MEMORY

of

WILBERT SCHEFFLER

January 28, 1939 - September 26, 1982

"No amount of experimentation can ever prove me right; a single experiment may at any time prove me wrong"

-Einstein

By the same author:

Fisherman's World
Fishing in America
Hunter's World
Hunting in America
Hunting Upland Birds
Modern Fresh & Salt Water Fly Fishing
The Part I Remember

THE PRACTICAL BOOK OF
TROUT FISHING

Charles F. Waterman

Drawings by Peter Corbin

Simon and Schuster | New York

Designed by Irving Perkins
Manufactured in the United States of America

1 2 3 4 5 6 7 8 9 10

Library of Congress Cataloging in Publication Data

Waterman, Charles F.
    The practical book of trout fishing.
    Bibliography: p.
    Includes index.
    1. Trout fishing. I. Title.
SH687.W36   799.1'7'55   76-54975

ISBN 0–671–22624–X

To Debie—
My Wife in Waders

CONTENTS

THE PRACTICAL BOOK OF TROUT FISHING

1
WHO FISHES FOR TROUT?

Who fishes for trout? The question can be answered in many ways, for the activity affords infinite variety. It can be an occasional brief diversion or a lifetime's obsessive avocation, and in either form it can be pursued around the world or on only a few hundred yards of local water. It can be explored as an intriguing science to endless depths of technicality or passed off as the most casual of pastimes. Yet if the angler chooses to investigate new avenues or seek new challenges, they can also take endless paths and innumerable directions. It is some sport.

This chapter will deal partly with what trout fishing is, and partly with who does or could do it, and if it rambles a bit you can blame the size of the subject as well as the way I write. It is addressed to the novice angler, but it represents judgments formed by over half a century of fishing experience, and if some of these have interest for more experienced anglers too, so much the better.

Trout fishing is not a very good way to seek fame and fortune. Trout fishermen are unlikely to become famous for their sport except among other trout fishermen, and some of the greatest of them are unknown a few miles from their chosen swatch of water. Nonetheless, the sport does not lack for heroes, for the pages of its ample literature are graced by a legion of skilled casters, erudite entomologists and dedicated seekers of great trout in far places.

Trout fishing can be social, secluded or even snobbish. Its traditions are the oldest in the angling sports, and its literature goes back through the centuries to a time when English was written differently and rod weights were estimated in pounds rather than ounces.

Fly fishing has long been regarded as a sport for ladies and gentlemen, although a fly rod can no more produce a gentleman than can an engraved shotgun. Yet admittedly, many famous and cultivated people have been devoted to fly fishing for trout—a fact that has produced some highly exclusive angling clubs and contributed more than slightly to the great cost of some trout and salmon waters. For all of this, good trout fishing need not be expensive in America. Although the best classic waters are greatly reduced by development, there are still free streams and lakes for all.

Angler plays a leaping rainbow trout in a meadow stream that flows past a barnyard. This is typical "scientific" trout water where small flies are the rule.

There are uncomplicated trout fishing, highly technical trout fishing and all grades between, just as there are various cults addicted to special tactics whose initiates consider themselves superior to all other practitioners. At one time, when the dry, or floating, trout fly first gained popularity in America after its long tenure in Great Britain, its devotees scorned any fly that sank. Then, to their horror, they were confronted by nymph fishermen, who had learned to fish a special kind of wet fly in a special and rather difficult way and argued, with some justification, that their method was the most advanced of all. When the nymph—a fly representing a water insect not ready to fly—made serious advances in England, it brought forth vigorous and sometimes pompous arguments concerning what was sporting and what wasn't, and the controversy is still, to some extent, going on although the original adversaries are long deceased.

"Hardware," generally meaning lures cast with spinning or plug-casting tackle, is considered boorish by some fishermen in some waters; but it has its place, as has "live bait" (generally meaning minnows) or worms, and sportsmen are not necessarily a product of their tools. Some of the most highly skilled operators are bait fishermen.

Despite its range of attractions, trout fishing is not for everyone. An angler who wants his picture in the newspaper would do better to stick to marlin or giant tuna, and few trout fishermen ever fill a freezer with their catches these days. For that matter, trout fishermen are now ringleaders in the movement to release fish once they are caught, and thousands of expert trout anglers never kill a fish. Indeed, there is an increasing number of trout streams in which it is illegal to keep fish that are caught—products of the "catch-and-release" concept.

Trout fishermen have long been the readers and writers of angling, and anyone digging into the history of sport fishing will find more about trout and salmon (all the same family) than about all other kinds of fishing put together. The long shelves of trout books would seem to indicate that the numbers of trout fishermen are a larger segment of the angling sport than they really are. In quantity of literature the trout were never challenged until the late twentieth century's boom in modern and scientific bass fishing, and in quality there is really no serious rival, even now.

A pastoral trout-fishing scene that fits the Izaak Walton pattern but is in Montana instead of England.

Trout fishermen have a reputation for contemplative nature loving, but there is much more to their sport than grassy meadow brooks and painted fences. Fishermen wade crashing torrents for big steelhead in catastrophic weather; mountaineers and horse packers labor far past timberline to catch 8-inch fish in seldom-visited trickles, for hard-bodied little trout have long since been planted in "cloud waters" by other trout lovers who hauled them there with great effort and even hardship. Atlantic salmon anglers spend years and fortunes on the best waters, wherever in the world they can be found. So trout fishermen don't necessarily fit the lazy grassy-bank philosophy commonly attributed to Izaak Walton.

If you visit some famous trout waters it is easy to assume that considerable worldly goods are a requirement for fishing. It's perfectly true that those who can afford to make regular pilgrimages to the best places try (often successfully) to buy or lease the water and build showplace homes within casting distance. And there is another kind of angler who also makes his home near the best water, albeit a type less noticed. He is a professional man—doctor, artist, lawyer, teacher—or an enterprising businessman who deliberately chooses a trout-fishing area in which to establish his career. Sometimes he does it the hard way by working at anything he can find while he gets started. In any case, he picks his home as much for its* angling possibilities as for its vocational potential.

All such people are a small minority of trout fishermen, but I mention them to indicate the level of devotion the sport can attract. It's a good selling point, perhaps, but I'm not in the selling business. Even though trout fishing is an obsession for me, it's only fair to point out that it's quite possible for people *not* to care about trout fishing, and a great many fine people don't. For every person who moves a thousand miles to be near a trout stream there is someone who lives on the bank of one, never wets a line and never will.

Most trout fishing requires skills that must be practiced, but once a bit of proficiency is acquired, an angler can maintain it in a few days of the year and get year-round enjoyment in studying the sport. If he becomes a fly tier he has an offshoot hobby which, in the case of some, can actually overshadow the main event. For many the challenges follow a certain evolutionary pattern, perhaps best described by Edward Ringwood Hewitt, a revered leader of the trout-and-salmon clan. At first, Hewitt said, he wanted to catch the most fish, then the largest fish—and finally, the most difficult fish.

That summary encompasses the creeds of thousands of trout fishermen, many of whom have followed Hewitt's pattern from youth to retirement. Some have even embraced his final philosophy, becoming ultimately less interested in catching fish than in having fish to catch; and thus a worthy proportion of trout fishermen develop into active conservationists.

There is a nearly automatic scale of values in trout fishing. An angler who spends most of his time on a meadow stream where a 12-inch fish is a rare prize will travel thousands of miles to a wide river where a 20-pound Atlantic salmon is not unusual. Yet in a way mysterious to the uninitiated, he can still go back to his little creek with the same enthusiasm he had when he left it. Its challenge will not have changed—and in fact, the 12-incher may be harder to catch than the 20-pounder.

Despite superficial similarities, the emphasis varies greatly in various types of trout fishing. For example, the techniques on some very clear and placid brooks are inextricably involved with the insect life that makes up the trout's diet. In order to catch such selective fish, the angler must "match the hatch" (copy the living insects with his flies) or go fishless. Such trout may be of almost any size, but they needn't be large to provide the fishing challenge, and in such waters it is generally necessary to use very light leaders. Thus, a one-pound trout hooked on a leader that tests only a pound is probably harder to land than a 10-pounder hooked on a leader testing 10 pounds. There is much more chance of human error with the lighter material, even if the fish is small.

So the fisherman who plays a fish with very light gear is not necessarily handicapping himself—if he used anything else, he probably couldn't hook the fish in the first place, for heavier tackle would scare it away. And his connection to the fish is tenuous at best, since the hook he uses might measure no more than $\frac{1}{16}$ inch across.

At the other extreme you'd find something like wet-fly steelhead fishing on the larger rivers of the Northwest—a sort of casting tournament with fish as prizes. There is no hatch to match, and the fly, a very simple pattern, must be weighted and tied on a large hook. Steelhead fishermen have reputations as the best distance casters of all, and their techniques and equipment have been accepted eagerly by other trout seekers who need a little extra reach now and then. In heavy steelhead water, wading is an athletic achievement, and some of the best steelhead fishing is found in remote sections where travel is an adventure in itself. Similar methods are used on some rivers where the quarry may be large brown, rainbow or cutthroat trout.

This book is devoted mainly to the use of fly tackle—not that other methods are unsporting, but because the majority of the most serious trout fishermen use flies. There are master anglers in spinning and plug-casting as well as in fly fishing, but the expert fly fisherman will have the basic knowledge for the other methods. If an angler chooses to use fly equipment only he need never get any

Trout fishermen travel to the most beautiful places in the world. Here Fred Terwilliger fishes the head of a river in Argentina.

other kind of tackle, although there are cases in which other gear will be more successful.

Now is the time for some very loose definitions. Not, perhaps, dictionary definitions, but common terms without which you won't understand what trout fishermen are talking about. Some grizzled veterans may not be in close agreement on all of my terminology, but we must start somewhere, and if you accept these definitions you won't be far off. I go into this because I have seen intelligent people completely befuddled by what appears to be angling mumbo jumbo—as confused as the baseball fan who is confronted for the first time with British cricket jargon.

Bait generally means some natural food, angleworms being the best-known. Where legal, salmon eggs are a popular bait, either in cluster or fished singly, and are bought in jars. *Single-egging*, of course, requires a very small hook. Real frogs and insects are also bait, as are pieces of fish. If only part of a fish is used it is commonly termed *cut bait*. Generally, *live bait* refers to whole small fish. The term *minnow* is commonly used to mean any small fish, although, technically, a minnow is a special kind of fish.

Artificial flies are never called bait, though some of the artificials cast with spinning or plug-casting rigs are occasionally called casting baits.

A *lure* is an artificial attraction which may or may not represent a particular living creature. Generally speaking, a trout fly is not termed a lure, even though one that resembles nothing in particular could be said to fit the definition. Spoons, spinners and artificial *plugs* are lures, whether they're cast with a fly rod or with a spinning outfit. A man casting a small spinner with a fly rod isn't considered to be fly-fishing by some definitions, even though everything except the lure is exactly the same.

Hardware refers to spoons, spinners and plugs, generally cast with spinning gear or "conventional" turning-spool reels. Hardware is also trolled from boats and sometimes takes the form of large *attractors* which precede a small lure or bait. The attractor brings the fish to the scene and he takes the smaller item.

A *wet fly* is one that is fished submerged and generally considered to represent a natural insect that has drowned. Here the plot thickens, for a *nymph*, which is intended to represent a living water insect that has not yet matured and cannot fly, is also fished underwater and thus is a wet, even though it is often considered different from the common wet fly. As you can see, the definition of wet flies and nymphs is hopelessly confused.

A *dry fly* is one that represents an insect (usually a living one) floating on the surface, and when fished in current is usually allowed to drift with little or no motion added by the rod and leader. The fly-rod *bug*, also a floater, is used primarily for bass rather than for trout and is generally manipulated with the rod.

The *streamer* is generally considered a special kind of wet "fly," although it actually represents a small fish and gets its underwater movement from current, line manipulation or both.

Though all of these definitions are rather vague and there is much overlapping, they are a reasonable key to trout-fishing parlance.

Now let's discuss how these different kinds of baits, lures and flies relate to fishing. Artificials go back for centuries, but it's quite possible that angleworms have caught more trout than any other attraction since time began. Although they can require a great deal of skill, worms are typically a beginner's bait, and advanced fishermen tend to use only artificial lures or flies. In fact, the "garden hackle" is something of a joke to the elite, and since there are conditions in which it is necessary for success, such fishermen simply avoid those times and places. Nonetheless, some expert users of artificial flies do employ worms under certain circumstances. When water is very muddy in early season or after heavy rains, lures or flies may not produce, and it's worms or nothing. The fellow with a short vacation who is faced with muddy water is likely to hunt a good place to dig.

Then there are some small streams so choked with brush that it is virtually impossible to cast any artificial, and dangling a worm between the overhanging branches is about the only thing that will work. This fishing is especially productive with the eastern brook trout (no longer confined to the East), but it works with all other varieties as well if the conditions are right.

One disadvantage with worms is that a large percentage of the fish take the hook so deeply it is difficult to release them unharmed. This is true to some extent with many other forms of bait. Most artificials are less damaging, as they are almost invariably rejected by the fish before being swallowed.

"Hardware" will work at times in almost any stream or lake where there is room to cast and retrieve it, and spoons and spinners come in all sizes. It is especially important in fishing for the Pacific salmons and steelhead trout, but it works in tiny brooks when appropriate tackle is used.

Dry flies are seldom useful except on clear water. Wet flies, nymphs and streamers work in both clear and murky, or "off-color," water, as do spoons and spinners. Some years ago it was common to say that a stream was "good dry-fly water," generally meaning that it was not too turbulent and quite clear. Of late, dry flies have been used more and more on swift, bumpy water, but there's no doubt that some streams simply aren't good for dries. Dry flies appeal to fish that get a large share of their nourishment from insects, and some streams produce a wide variety of insect hatches. In other waters, and in most streams at some times, nearly all of the food is found near the bottom and dry flies simply do not work. Knowing when and where they will catch fish is an important aspect of trout-fishing expertise. We'll look into that later.

A great many rising trout are viewed through bifocals, for the sport can be enjoyed to a ripe age. However, if you go to the rushing big rivers the fishermen tend to be younger, for labor is greater. Older anglers tend toward the streams that are easier to wade and where the casting is less arduous. Then too, we oldsters like to believe we've reached the stage of wanting the most difficult fish, and placid streams have a reputation for them, sometimes justified.

When can serious trout fishing begin? I do not believe that a 6-year-old who catches trout with bait or with flies in easy pools is necessarily on his way to advanced angling. His juvenile achievements are somewhat apart from later endeavor, even though a love for the outdoors can begin early. I've seen very few youngsters who found their way to a life of trout before their middle teens, and many have been pushed too hard by parents and grandparents who were sure you couldn't start too early in building a gentleman

Trout fishermen don't always wade in wild water. These are casting from a slowly drifting boat on a placid river.

angler. A kid who has fly patterns forced upon him when he'd rather be skipping rocks is likely to be an early dropout.

And it may be heresy, but I have never been impressed by the effects of children's trout-fishing contests staged with hungry hatchery trout in city-park pools. Somehow the experience of jerking out stupid fish, dragging them to death on a string and then measuring them for prizes doesn't seem to produce sterling sportsmen. It probably doesn't do much harm either, but catching a winning fish on canned corn, a marshmallow or a worm is a way to win a contest and nothing more.

A youngster should be exposed to trout fishing as soon as it's convenient, but it isn't something that can be given him like an injection; if he must be persuaded, forced or coaxed, the chances are he's not ready and may never be. Fortunately, not every child will be a trout fisherman.

A beginning boy or girl should be given adequate and balanced tackle with which he or she can catch trout, given a little skill. Doting parents who hand a child a $500 fly rod made by one of the old masters in the hope it will spur him on to angling greatness are probably doing more harm than good. Part of the game is learning to appreciate good tackle, and to acquire it with some effort when it can be of help. A genuine Stradivarius is not much of an aid during the first few music lessons. Many of the finest trout fishermen to whom money is no object use modestly priced gear.

At the other end of the angling age bracket are elderly people who look for a relaxing hobby and have an abundance of time to practice it. If they have some previous experience in some sort of light-tackle fishing they are good candidates, but if they have never "found time" to fish before, chances that they will become trout anglers are very remote indeed. Anyone who has never found the time, regardless of how much effort is required, to do some fishing before retirement is unlikely to put much into it when his work is over. He might become a tackle collector and a reader of fishing literature, but I strongly doubt if the wading-and-casting spark is there.

This retirement fishing scene is a sort of specialty of mine, as I have taken part in numerous fishing clinics in communities where many of the participants were retired. Some of them were looking

Who fishes for trout? Though there are no children present, in other respects this group is a reasonable cross section; they are giving rapt attention to Leon Chandler of the Cortland Line Company at a conclave of the Federation of Fly Fishermen.

very hard for a pleasant way to spend their time and felt that retirement would somehow completely change their viewpoint. Thus, a couple who had been addicted to bridge during their productive days and had no interest in the outdoors at all felt that things would now be different, not realizing that although they might live in a new area and have new friends, they are still the people who played bridge (or whatever) in all of their spare time. And their attitude toward fishing is generally fairly passive. Get the tackle and go to the right place, they think, and everything will work out. Whatever else trout fishing may be, it is not a completely effortless pastime, and I have to refer to the tiresome fact that you get out of it just about what you put into it.

And with older people there is a more complicated situation, involving men who have fished much of their lives and now, with retirement, are anxious to take their wives along. How, they ask, can they interest their wives in the sport, now that both of them have all the spare time they want? The truthful answer is that the chances of doing this are also pretty slim, though there are notable exceptions. I know one lady, now in her 70s, who began trout fishing to go with her husband when she was well into her 60s and became highly successful. She has not become more than an adequate caster, but she has more than made up for casting deficiencies with fish sense and delicacy of presentation.

But this is highly unusual, and the reasons are quickly explained. In most cases, the husband has done his fishing with other men while his wife has devoted her attention to the home, children and women friends she has acquired herself. He now asks her to completely change her interests, simply because he no longer works. Here is a fellow who may once have considered that getting away from his family was one of the attractions of fishing; now he decides to favor his wife with his steady company, even during the fishing she was never invited to share in prior years. He and she have a problem, and it will require a great deal of tolerance on both sides, especially the wife's. The chance of their becoming a fishing team is pretty skimpy. Remember that she has considered those outdoor magazines as living-room trash for 50 years.

Forgetting the retirement complexities, how about women as trout anglers? There are more all the time, but they still make up a very small part of the total. As to their ability, there is no question,

Women anglers can be highly skilled, especially where delicacy and finesse are required. This is Mrs. Ben Williams.

especially in fishing that requires patience and delicacy. Some of the best small-stream anglers I know are women. Not many of them go for the long casts and hard wading of bigger water.

For the most part, women do not have the fishing drive that men have, but there has been a great deal of feminine interest in the outdoors of late, and the future may be different. Women show less interest in tackle and technique, and few of them like to practice casting, study tackle catalogs or read angling literature. This is due in part to the patronizing attitude of their men—in which we must acknowledge the role of some potent male chauvinism, for men do not want women to equal or surpass them in angling. A man with a wife who consistently outfishes his friends will soon find his male fishing friends becoming scarce. Believe it.

I find men less considerate toward women anglers than they are toward other men, and on public waters I have watched women get crowded out of the better spots. In mixed fishing groups, women are often relegated to the least productive waters, probably not so much through conscious unfairness as through a male feeling that the women's fishing simply isn't very important. Most women seem to accept this, and I cannot explain why. Perhaps the ladies have a hard time getting past their own impression that the outdoors is fundamentally a man's world in which they are some sort of provisional guests.

I don't wish to labor the male–female fishing thing, but it's highly complex. For example, a lady wishing to learn the rudiments of fly casting will find plenty of males eager to lend her advice and instruction—to a point. When she passes the beginner stage and starts to acquire a few opinions and skills of her own, I note that the men disappear into the willows. And it is embarrassing to me when I see a lady angler carefully avoiding fish lest she catch more than her share, because there is no reason why a woman cannot fish as well as or better than a man. Part of the situation is the women's fault for accepting it, but it's mostly a male ego problem. (Right now I am assuming that nearly all of my readers are men—something I earnestly wish were not the case.)

Women are not self-starters. There must be a few, but I cannot name a single expert woman angler who was not steered into it by a man. I know a number of lady anglers who fish alone or with other women, but invariably they have been started by male friends, their husbands or their fathers.

And mere association with the equipment and the locale isn't enough to make women want to fish. For example, some of the world's very best fly tiers are women, but few ever take up fishing. Let's be specific. Dan Bailey's Fly Shop is located a few blocks from the famous Yellowstone River, but of the hundreds of good feminine fly tiers who have been or are currently employed by Bailey's, I do not know of three who have taken any interest in fly fishing. And most of the *famous* fly tiers are men who took up fly construction because they liked to fish.

Trout fishing in most cases requires that the angler show some skills on his own. I have known deep-sea fishermen who became well known as experts through the efforts of efficient boat captains while the "experts" themselves did little but pump and reel in prize catches. It doesn't work often with trout, especially stream fish. It could work where large trout are caught by trolling.

Where physical condition and strength are concerned, fly fishing for trout (and we're going to concentrate on that, even though we touch on other methods as well) meets a rather strange barrier. It's simply this: The beginner frequently uses muscles that aren't disciplined and he does everything the hard way. He works hard for mediocre results, and no matter how much he is told that things will get easier, he tends to think he has taken on a job of work. Then this problem is compounded when he reaches a point where he actually casts well, but his timing is off just enough so that he is forcing things.

"I can do it," he says to himself, "but it's a lot of tiresome work." So he tends to quit just before things get easy.

Believe me, the exertion required in efficient fly casting is so slight that a good fisherman's feet should get tired long before his arms, even when he is using a heavy outfit on big water. And he labors even less with light gear on small streams.

True, there is more work involved if you actually need great distance, but even that is much more a matter of timing than a matter of strength. Some years ago, the American men's champion at salmon-fly distance casting weighed only 145 pounds, though that contest is considered the most strenuous of fly-casting events, requiring two-handed rods that resemble surf sticks. (In fact, some of the distance rods of that day were actually made from the same glass blanks used in surf casting.)

It is nonetheless true that strength is an aid, for a strong arm may not get tired as quickly as a frail one in the learning process. It is also true that a linebacker might prefer heavier equipment than a stenographer, and there are some ultrapowerful rods that would not work in all-day fishing for slight people. However, there is no phase of trout fishing that *demands* tackle too heavy for persons weighing 85 pounds or more, and much of the best angling requires nothing

Hiking fishermen operate in some of America's wildest backcountry. These anglers, equipped for several days in the Rockies, are headed for mountaintop lakes and "cloud trout."

heavier than a whisk broom. If it is done right, the fishing process is a matter of timing rather than strength, and if it hurts you're probably doing it wrong.

There is trout fishing that undeniably requires rugged physiques, but this is not because of the fishing itself but because of the effort required in reaching the scene. Backpacking into high trout lakes can be exhausting, and even horse packing into backcountry can place a premium on physical conditioning. Where wading is involved, there are some pretty adventurous rivers, some of them for athletic types, but there is other excellent fishing where knee boots will suffice, and there are some brooks fished from dry banks.

The wading itself can add to the fun of fishing, and some anglers say much of trout fishing's appeal lies in "getting in there with the fish." But there is leisurely boat fishing too, and many canoe enthusiasts combine the two sports in both placid and white water.

There are fly-fishing buffs who collect tackle and seldom use it, and some big-city sporting-goods dealers say that their lunchtime business with its little groups of people talking trout is the highlight of their business day. There was a time when I had a bit of scorn for what I called "lunchtime anglers," but I know now that some of them enjoy themselves as much as or more than steady operators who spend all their vacations, weekends and stolen hours on the stream.

I no longer smirk at the fellow who pulled up a rented automobile near a stream where my wife and I were flailing away and came through the tall grass and weeds in his business suit, wanting to know how the fishing was. Although he said he was on a business trip and had no time to fish himself, I could tell he had something else on his mind. Finally, with the friendliness that seems to be contagious among fishermen, he said he wanted to show me his flies, and with condescending courtesy I followed him to the car's trunk, which he opened with a flourish.

That trunk was nearly filled with transparent plastic boxes full of trout flies—hundreds of them—many of them tied by masters of the art. I saw no rod, and I did not ask him why he had happened to take such a selection on a business trip. He talked rapidly of patterns, modifications of patterns and specialized flies made for distant waters I wish I had fished. He commented on hooks and leaders, but mostly on the exquisite flies themselves. When he finally glanced at his watch, he said he had to be going and left in an urgent cloud of dust, leaving me standing in patched waders and grubby vest at the roadside, thinking what a strange man he was. But I doubt now, some years later, that I had any more fun fishing that day than he had in showing his flies, some of which he had tied himself.

I know another man who fishes with antique tackle and owns a collection going back to the beginnings of American trout angling. I know a fine fisherman who fishes with no fly he has not tied himself and will accept gifts of flies with courtesy, deigning to copy them but unwilling to get the originals wet.

So the question of who fishes for trout is very difficult to answer, and there is no mold that fits them all.

2

INTRODUCING THE TROUTS

Having dealt at some length with what trout fishing is and who trout fishermen are, we can now turn to some basic facts about the fish themselves and their ecology. Obviously, some knowledge of fish and their habits is essential to the angler, but it can also be much more than a means to an end. Master anglers never stop learning, and some of them eventually find that studying the fish can be just as much fun as catching them.

There's no shortage of literature on our subject. In fact, there are shelves of technical works, most of them well researched and reflecting years of stream experience. Unfortunately, they sometimes speak in the strange tongue of the addict, with the basics stuffed in only as brief appendages to pet theories and learned conclusions, and too often they are exclusively concerned with narrow specific areas.

No one can be a master fisherman on all trout and salmon waters. A favorite coffee-cup theme of the specialist is the way a California steelheader has been humbled on a New England brook or the way a meadow-stream wizard has recoiled in horror from the stinging spray of a mountain torrent. There's a great variety in trout fishing, and there's no disgrace in someone's preferring a certain kind of it; that's no reason to be intolerant. Also, let's not make any flat statements about such-and-such a trout's being stupider or wiser than his peers. Many factors are involved when a trout is easy to catch or hard to catch.

For example, the brown trout is generally considered the most perceptive of all and is most likely to feed on surface insects, leading to delicate fishing. The rainbow is supposedly easier to fool, and the larger ones are less likely to feed on the surface, but in an insect-filled meadow stream containing both kinds they'll behave much the same as the browns. Big browns and rainbows living in deep lakes may feed mainly on small fish. So the type of water and the kind of food it affords has almost as much bearing, where method is concerned, as the species of the fish. The cutthroat trout of the West isn't supposed to be a difficult fish to fool with artificial flies, but when found in slow, very clear waters along with brown trout it can be almost as difficult to hook. So if your flies take cutthroat trout in Yellowstone Park, there is no reason why they won't take brown trout in Pennsylvania.

Before discussing the fishes we're most concerned with individually, I'd like to make a couple of general points, starting with the distinction between trout and salmon. This is one of the most confusing matters we have to deal with, but by putting it in early we can make things go more smoothly later on. Most beginning trout fishermen don't quite understand it, and if you don't either, don't worry about it.

A good fact to know at the very beginning is that basically, the trouts and the salmons belong to the same tribe. The Atlantic salmon has a special niche today because it grows large and is often difficult and expensive to come by, but it is hooked by the same methods that work on much smaller fish with very light tackle in running water. It is very different from the Pacific salmons and behaves more like the steelhead, which is really a rainbow trout that spends part of its life at sea in much the same manner. The Pacific salmons, which die after spawning, are often sought by sport fishermen in salt water or in the Great Lakes and are caught less often by fly anglers. There is little offshore sport fishing for Atlantic salmon.

One other fish, the grayling, must be discussed in any comprehensive coverage of the subject of trout. Although it isn't a trout, it is caught by trout methods by trout fishermen, and so we'll add a word about it later. That's as far as we'll go from "trout" in this classification. Now I'll list the best-known fishes and give some of their special characteristics. Note that two or more of these species will often be found in the same water, and there is a tendency for their behavior to be quite similar in the same habitat.

In describing the trouts, we'll do so from a fisherman's viewpoint, leaving true ichthyology to the professional biologists or to anglers who want to delve further in other books.

EASTERN BROOK TROUT

The "eastern" part of the name doesn't really apply anymore, for this fish has now been introduced over much of the continent. How-

Small brook trout lie in the snow beside a high-country creek. They are greatly prized as food.

ever, it was the trout that met the first white settlers in the East, and for a long time all other American trouts were measured by it. It demands cold, clean water and for that reason has suffered greatly from civilization's changes.

The "brookie" is *generally* easier to fool than either a brown or a rainbow trout, but here we must remember our rules about judging fish qualities. It is one of the best as food; but this quality, remember, is partly a matter of habitat. Clean cold water makes for firm flesh and good taste. Brilliantly colored, the brook trout has worm-like markings, or vermiculations, on its back.

Brookies thrive in many rocky waters, but are also happy over dark mud bottoms, and they often live in very small creeks. A great deal of brook trout fishing is for small fish in brushy spots, and some of the most productive fishermen use earthworms as bait. Brookies will take all of the attractions used for any trout, but are not quite so prone to take floating flies as are some others. Gaudy fly patterns are popular for them. They do not often jump when hooked.

At present, the largest brook trout consistently caught on light tackle are found in Canada, and the big fish generally come from big water—a fact with other trouts as well. Brook trout have been replaced by rainbow and brown trout in many areas because the latter are able to withstand warmer water of less purity. Under some conditions the brookie is especially prone to overcrowd and become stunted. Some of the best wilderness brookie fishing is now found in the Rocky Mountains, where man's activities have been minimal.

This is a fall spawner and is technically listed as a "char," along with mackinaw trout and the Dolly Varden. The arctic char is generally encountered only by wilderness anglers in the Far North. The char group of fishes has specific anatomical characteristics which are unimportant to the fisherman and are not noticeable except through careful examination.

RAINBOW TROUT

Rainbows were originally western fish, and the steelhead is simply a rainbow trout that goes to sea. In evolution, the inland fish probably evolved from the saltwater traveler, and this includes both landlocked fish and those which have an open avenue to the ocean.

The "rainbow" name comes from a red stripe along the side; but in some waters the color is not distinct, and fresh-run steelhead (those just in from the ocean) are predominantly silver. Rainbows have been extremely adaptable; they are very successful as hatchery fish, and they can withstand warmer waters than the other trouts. Hence, they have been introduced around the globe.

They reach great size in lakes and large rivers, as both steelhead and resident trout, and are caught by every method known to trout fishing. In some streams they can be hooked only with great delicacy, but in some lakes they are taken with heavy trolling tackle. Call the rainbow the most democratic trout of all. The 'bow has a reputation as the hardest fighter of the list, and it is a great jumper. It is a winter or early-spring spawner. The steelhead resembles the Atlantic salmon more than the Pacific salmon, even though the Pacific coast is its best-known home, and it is believed that the Atlantic salmon and Pacific steelhead come from a common ancestry that lived when the oceans had a more southerly connection over what is now Canada. The rainbows that leave the Great Lakes to spawn in rivers are called "steelheads" locally, and this complicates

A sinking line and large rubber-legged nymph were used for this rainbow in a deep lake. The tackle is heavy for handling a big shooting head and throwing a wind-resistant fly against the wind.

the term. With that logic, any rainbow that spends most of its time in a lake and then enters tributary streams for spawning would be a steelhead too.

BROWN TROUT

This one is not an American native at all, having been introduced from Europe in the 1880s. It's noted for feeding on small surface insects after it reaches a size at which most other species have turned principally to underwater feeding. This means that large brown trout are frequently fished with very delicate tackle and presentation, and the old term of "scientific angling" is well applied to the brown. The fish is also called the "Loch Leven trout" and the "German brown," those names coming from the sources of the original stock brought to America.

As with most other fish, there are times and places when the brown trout is caught by crude methods, but the use of chunks of sucker meat or large baitfish in some cases does not detract from the advanced skills demanded under other conditions.

Although the rainbow can withstand warmer water for short peri-

Giant brown trout from Missouri River displayed by Bud Schlect of Montana. This male (note hooked jaw) was in full spawning colors in late fall and took a large streamer.

ods, the brown trout is noted for survival where other trouts fail, and warmed and polluted rivers sometimes contain big browns that have outlasted lesser fish. There has been bitter controversy about brown trout, some believing that very large ones are unlikely to be caught and that they consume too many of the smaller fish. "Cannibalism" is a frequent term in discussion of trout populations.

The brown is a good fighter, although seldom as agile as the rainbow. It jumps less under most conditions. It spawns in the fall, which leads to catches of large specimens at that time of year, usually with large streamers or lures.

CUTTHROAT TROUT

Originally confined to the West, the cutthroat trout has not spread its range as much as the rainbow. It gets its name from red slashes on the underside of the gill area, and it hybridizes with the rainbow. It seldom jumps when hooked and is not considered so hard a fighter as the rainbow or brown. It is famous in the Yellowstone Park area, one of the greatest of trout-fishing centers, and was originally the only trout found there. It spawns in the spring.

Cutthroat trout, the original "native" species of the West, caught on dry flies. The "cutt" can often be caught easily, but can be insistent upon small flies at times. These came from a small stream in high country.

A hooked grayling in the extremely clear water of a Yukon river. This one took a dry fly. Grayling tend to follow a fly downstream before striking and sometimes like it moved cross-current. "Drag" is sometimes a help in grayling fishing.

GRAYLING

Grayling are not properly a trout, but they are found in similar waters and are fished with the same methods. Their habitat resembles that of the brook trout and is even more demanding. Water purity and coldness are essential, and grayling are becoming a rarity in the contiguous states, although they are plentiful in Canada and Alaska. In the Rockies, grayling now run quite small and are pretty hard to find. They are delicate feeders and take artificial flies well. There's little agreement about the appearance of fish, but the grayling with its huge dorsal fin and iridescent tints is a popular candidate as a beauty winner.

Grayling were once plentiful in the Michigan area but were replaced by the brook trout, much as the brook trout has later been replaced by the rainbow and brown. Grayling do not build nests, or "redds," as do most trout.

DOLLY VARDEN

The Dolly Varden, also called the "bull trout," is scorned by many trout fishermen and is generally (not always) taken with rather coarse tackle, preferring bait and hardware to flies. It's primarily a western resident and becomes very large, especially as a sea-run variety. It spawns in the fall in running water.

LAKE TROUT

Generally caught by trolling with deep-going lures, the lake trout, or mackinaw, is primarily a big-water fish that grows very large in cold depths. However, there are locations where lakers are taken with a variety of light casting tackle just after ice goes out on northern lakes, especially in Canada and Alaska. The typical habitat is in water of low fertility.

GOLDEN TROUT

The brilliantly hued western golden trout, an offshoot of the rainbow, is found in high-altitude waters of the western mountains, and its range has been greatly widened by transplanting. Originally, it was found only in a small area of California. An eastern golden, a completely different fish found in deep lakes, has been near extinction for some time but remains in small numbers in New England. Both of these trouts are pretty much, at present, in the special-dividend category.

ATLANTIC SALMON

Considered the king of game fishes by its followers, the Atlantic salmon nearly disappeared from the U.S. Atlantic coast despite the unbelievable plenty of colonial days. However, it has maintained good populations in Canada as well as in Europe and is coming back on the New Engand coast through stringent regulation of commercial fishing at sea. A landlocked form runs smaller but is a sporting fish in both New England and Canada.

Atlantic salmon are often called the kings among game fish and are frequently caught on very small flies. These small fresh-run specimens were caught in New Brunswick.

In most American sport-fishing rivers the Atlantic salmon is legally fished only with flies. It spawns in fresh water and does not necessarily die afterward as do the Pacific salmons. It deserves some extra attention because of its special terminology, some of which is shared with other salmons and trouts. When the very young salmon first becomes active and is absorbing its egg sac it is called an *alevin*. As a fully formed small fish in fresh water it is a *parr,* and when it first migrates to salt water at the age of 2 or 3 years it is a *smolt*. If it returns to fresh water after only one winter at sea it is a *grilse,* and a fish that has spawned and is returning to the sea is a *kelt* or *black salmon.* The term "parr" is frequently applied to other species, and small trout that retain the special coloration of very young fish are said to still have their parr marks.

Most of the trouts spawn in a manner similar to that of the Atlantic salmon, the female clearing an area on suitable gravel bottom and depositing her eggs there and the male fish then coming alongside to fertilize them. After the eggs are deposited they are generally covered by the female with loose gravel, but the extent of the cover-up operation varies with the species. The term *redd* is applied to trout nests, or beds.

PACIFIC SALMON

The several varieties of Pacific salmon spawn in freshwater rivers and die shortly afterward. In the past, they were almost always caught with fairly heavy tackle, but fly fishermen have recently perfected efficient techniques. As a light-tackle fish, the coho, or silver salmon, is most popular. The entire Pacific salmon picture has changed with the dramatic introduction of cohos into the Great Lakes, and artificial propagation has proved successful where natural reproduction will not work.

Having looked at the principal species individually, let's now consider some simplified and generalized facts about trout and salmon. Although I've briefly described the major kinds, remember that there are subspecies and specially adapted fish that simply refuse to follow general descriptions. For example, the spectacular western golden trout tends to go back to the more common colors of the typical rainbow when brought to lower altitudes.

And the saltwater business: Nearly all kinds of trout have saltwater versions. Even some brook trout become "salters" when they spend part of their lives in the ocean. Other trouts have different saltwater names. The Atlantic and Pacific salmons go great distances in the oceans, while some of the other salmonids range only short spaces from the tidal river mouths. Fresh and salt water are closely tied together in ancient evolutions of the fishes, and freshwater varieties have developed through becoming landlocked by natural forces. A confusing factor is the variety of local names tacked to the migratory fish.

It is almost impossible to identify trouts by their colors alone. In muddy water, trout tend to have light colors, but in clear water with dark, muddy bottoms they are likely to become especially dark, and most trout from deep holes in rivers are likely to have dark colors regardless of the bottom type. Fish from the ocean tend to be silvery overall and then resume their "native" colors once they return to fresh water. A fresh-run steelhead is silvery, but just before spawning it may be quite dark with a blood-red stripe. Although the Great

Lakes are considered fresh water, they can produce the silvery coloring of steelhead. And to make matters more complex, saltiness is a relative condition. It's not necessary for the trout fisherman to understand all of these vagaries of markings, but he should know they exist.

There are long arguments about the fighting qualities of fish. The rainbow, generally considered the wildest runner and jumper of all, can be sluggish when fresh from a hatchery pool. The Atlantic salmon loses some of its fight as it nears its spawning area upstream, spent and battered. A Pacific salmon at the end of its upstream run is almost dead weight on a line. If water is too cold, trout become sluggish, and if it becomes too warm they do the same. Fish that are either too cold or too warm feed very little, and their digestive action is slowed. Generally speaking, a well-conditioned trout has a deep body and a relatively small head, but males tend to develop long jaws which are hooked into a "kipe."

There is confusion about underfed trout. Overcrowded fish or fish in water of very low fertility may be highly energetic even though dwarfed, having adapted to their surroundings. Size is a poor measure of a trout's age. A large trout that loses much of its food supply becomes sluggish and is very different from the smaller fish of the same age that grew up in slim pickings.

MANAGEMENT

Hatchery production of trout and salmon has advanced tremendously in very recent years and has raised its own problems. The perennial debate is whether large numbers of catchable trout should be used to replenish a supply in heavily fished waters. Of late, this has been complicated by surveys indicating that adding hatchery fish to water that already maintains a "normal" population will actually decrease the numbers of native fish. The residents seem to disappear.

In waters where there is no natural reproduction the "put-and-take" concept appears. This is simply a matter of raising fish in hatcheries and releasing them where they will, it is hoped, survive until they can be caught out. Perhaps none of them will live there very long, but they can provide fishing where otherwise there would

Modern trout philosophy sometimes calls for releasing the big ones as well as the little ones. Chester Marion is here making sure the subject is ready to travel on his own.

be none. No two streams or lakes are exactly alike, and in some areas this is a rousing success; in others it is questionable or obviously wasteful. Hatchery fish are expensive when they are raised to a catchable size, but flat value judgments on them are inappropriate. Some waters will produce huge trout or salmon but do not provide spawning areas that will work.

Hatchery fish are inclined to be naive bumpkins when first re-leased, leading to the "tourist fisherman" debate. Skilled trout anglers may consider them no challenge, but those engaged in the tourist trade are happy that casual fishermen on brief vacations can catch some fish. "Following the hatchery truck" is the extreme in put-and-take fishing and has been widely practiced. Generally speaking, the longer a hatchery fish survives in the wild the more difficult it is to fool. Some strains of hatchery fish are better than others, and most of our trout fishing is the result of plantings at some time or place.

There are planted waters that accommodate elbow-to-elbow fishermen on opening day, and although the master angler may scorn such activities, the fact that thousands of people seem to be enjoying themselves is irrefutable. It's an extension of the tourist-fisherman concept and often comes down to matching brief enjoyment for the many against more tranquil pleasures for the expert few.

The greatest losses in trout fishing are a matter of habitat. Pollution by foreign matter is much publicized, but by no means the only problem. Thermal pollution of overwarmed water is less dramatic and can be produced by the elimination of forest cover, allowing too much sun on the water. Damming or diversion can slow water to the point that it warms excessively. Industrial discharge of warmed water, even though it is relatively pure, can destroy trout habitat.

Good trout streams must have meanders. A straight channel not only carries water away too quickly but also lacks the cover for trout and for the things the trout eats. Trout live among rocks, logs, stumps and living vegetation and against undercut banks. Straighten the channel and much of this cover disappears. A straightened channel carries a quick flood burden that is destructive of cover for a brief period; then, since the water has been hurried away, a drought can virtually destroy the flow.

Too much silt obliterates the stone-and-gravel bottom essential to the growth of trout food, and silt can enter a stream either because of land cultivation or because forests have been cut, allowing the land to erode. In agricultural areas, irrigation water is removed from trout streams at the very time of year it is needed. Stream bed is exposed and the remaining water is warmed exclusively. "Returned" irrigation water sometimes causes silting, and it may be too far downstream to be of much help to a drought-struck watercourse.

Highway construction has been deadly, more so than appears at first, because highways follow the valleys and rivers in mountainous areas and hundreds of miles of native streams are changed. A new stream bed may never have the fishy potential of an established one, and it will take years at best for it to match the original's production of trout food.

Power dams are spectacular destroyers of trout habitat, eliminating thousands of miles of running water, and the most publicized have been built on the giant steelhead and salmon rivers of the Pacific coast. Fish ladders and hatcheries have helped restore runs, but much has been lost, and man's continuing quest for power bodes no good for the future. Even where reservoirs have maintained good fishing of another type, stream fishing is eliminated, and this brings up another aspect of the recreation picture.

There is a basic conflict of interest between the builders of dams and lakeside family resorts and the serious fisherman. A lake brings forth large pleasure boats and miles of waterfront for summer homes or year-round residences, and in many cases it creates thriving resort communities. The lake fishing may be largely trolling in trout country, but it can still appeal to large numbers of vacationers. Where warmer rivers have been dammed, bass fishing has often boomed on the impoundments, and although Southerners lament the loss of their rivers, it must be admitted that there's more fishing for more people since the lakes came.

Trout are considered "cold-water" species, and though a cold lake may harbor many large trout even after the streams are lost, we may as well face the fact that the best trout angling is nearly always in running water. (In saying "best," I am again invoking that ancient term, "scientific fishing.") Thus while nearly all highly skilled trout fishermen *sometimes* fish in lakes, they spend much more of their time on running water. Once a stream is dammed it cannot be revived, and we cannot afford further loss of stream fishing.

THE INSECTS AND THEIR IMITATIONS

You cannot become a trout fisherman without learning something about insect life. However, while trout fishermen sometimes become true entomologists (because so much of the finest angling is concerned with imitation of natural insects through the use of artificial flies), there are other superb anglers who can name very few insects and know no Latin nomenclature at all. The detailed study of natural insects can become an intriguing offshoot of trout fishing, but it is not necessary.

Most of the insects that trout feed on actually spend much of their lives in the water as *nymphs,* or larvae, before they hatch into flying insects. Most people who find their automobile radiators clogged with "bugs" when they drive near trout streams know that those things hang around the creeks, but have no idea that they are actually products of the water itself. You can find these immature insects under rocks, in the mud or clinging to vegetation underwater. When they mature as flying insects in great numbers, we have a *hatch*. Matching the hatch means simply that we employ a fly that looks much like the living insect. Sometimes this is simple and sometimes it is difficult or impossible, and that fascinating puzzle has brought about the thousands of named and unnamed patterns of flies.

Mayflies and their nymphs make up a major share of the trout flies imitated by fishermen, and the species of mayflies number in the hundreds. On some streams their hatches are well documented and studious fishermen know about what time of year to expect each variety, the fly sizes varying greatly from species to species.

The various mayfly life spans vary greatly, but the sequence goes about like this: mature mayflies deposit their eggs on the water, in which they hatch first into nymphs, little multilegged insects with gills. The nymphs spend the fall and winter underwater, feeding on small organisms. They then rise to the surface during the warm months and hatch, and a winged insect emerges from the nymphal shuck. This new fly, now called a *dun* or *subimago*, flies to a nearby resting place, where in about 24 hours it sheds its skin a second time, and the mature insect emerges, mates, deposits its eggs on the surface and dies. The final stage is called the *imago*—or the "spinner," because of the "dance of death" presented over the water by the mating insects.

Dry-fly anglers are primarily interested in the dun stage of the insect, but nymph and wet-fly users are often more successful when no flies are emerging. A mayfly spends much more time as a resident nymph than it does in its brief floating appearance as a dun. When trout are feeding on the surface or near it and a fisherman casts to their surface disturbances or to visible fish themselves, he is "fishing the rise." A few specialists abandon all other kinds of operations.

Caddis flies come in even more varieties than mayflies but are not nearly so widely imitated by dry flies. Caddis eggs are laid near or on the water, and the grublike larva (not called a nymph) frequently builds a protective case of sand or plant matter held to-

A giant stone fly shuck, left over from the preceding summer, is still present as a fall angler works a swift run.

gether by silk. Trout often eat case and all. When the mature fly emerges, it carries its wings folded back over its body. The mayflies carry their wings erect and float perkily atop the water while they dry—the critical moment for dry-fly imitations.

Mature stone flies also fold their wings down over their bodies. The females frequently lay their eggs by dipping the tips of their abdomens beneath the surface in flight. When the nymphs have matured, they crawl from the water and cling to stones or plants until the true fly emerges.

Most of the water-bred insects imitated by fishermen are covered by those three names—mayfly, caddis fly and stone fly. (We'll get to the tiny midges later.) If a fisherman refers to a "salmon fly" he is often speaking of a large specific form of the stone fly, and he may never have heard of the broader classification. The name Green Drake is applied to one of the larger common mayflies. In many cases fishermen refer to the natural fly by the name of an artificial which imitates it, an efficient matter of getting the cart before the horse, and it's common to hear that a "Size 16" mayfly is hatching. That's simply the size of the hook that would take an artificial which would match the hatch.

Anyone can watch mature flies floating on the surface and see fish take them if conditions are right. Nymph activity is something else, since nymphs can be found anywhere between surface and bottom—and even farther down than that, because some nymphs are burrowers. And nymphs are taken anywhere between surface and bottom when trout are feeding. Some nymphs are highly active swimmers, and many are taken by trout while floating upward toward the surface before emerging as flies. If it's very near the surface, the resulting swirl is much like that made when the fish takes a floater. Other nymphs may be near the surface when they have no intention of hatching.

Certain types of streams are subject to regular hatches and become famous for it. Other waters, which carry just as many fish, will have little or no visible trout activity and a fisherman can have a highly successful day without so much as seeing a trout that isn't on his line. I'll speak of water types later.

Many anglers fish successfully for a lifetime without ever knowing the simple insect facts we've just considered; but they are worth knowing, even if you never study any further. (If this is the first you've read about trout fishing you probably feel the field is endless, and you're right.) Now, within this broad framework, let's discuss the general types of artificial flies, ignoring specific patterns. We can group them in four different categories:

A *dry fly* floats on the surface, and generally imitates an insect that has emerged from the water to fly and to lay its eggs. However, a few dry flies imitate some terrestrial insect that was hatched away from the water and has fallen into it, generally by accident. A grasshopper is a good example of that.

A *wet fly* usually indicates a flying insect that has died and has sunk beneath the surface.

An *artificial nymph* represents the immature stage of an insect that cannot yet use its wings and may be fished anywhere from the bottom to the surface. There is much overlap between wet flies and nymphs.

A *streamer* is generally fished beneath the surface, and though it is called a fly, it usually represents a small fish. In trout fishing, the streamer is seldom an attempt at exact imitation, although the size, general outline and color may be close to those of a specific species.

This broad classification of fly types will no doubt bring triumphant cries from nitpickers who are happy to catch somebody in

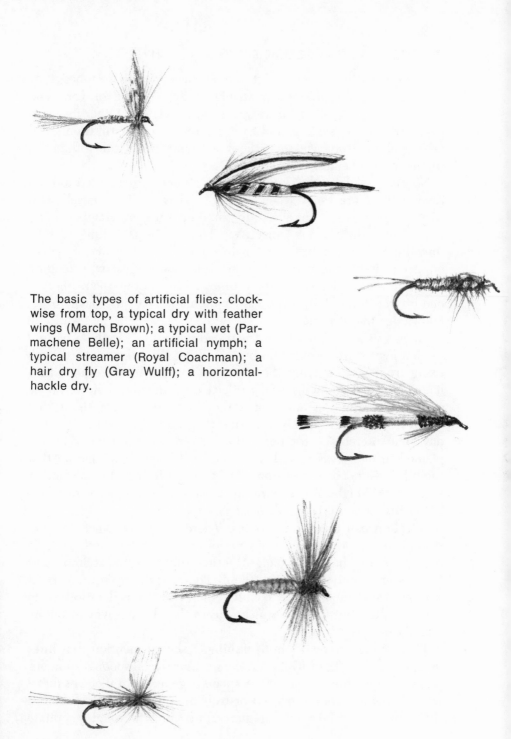

The basic types of artificial flies: clockwise from top, a typical dry with feather wings (March Brown); a typical wet (Parmachene Belle); an artificial nymph; a typical streamer (Royal Coachman); a hair dry fly (Gray Wulff); a horizontal-hackle dry.

oversimplification. Dozens of flies don't fit any of these types, they say. For example, a popular steelhead fly is made of yarn and mimics salmon eggs, a favorite steelhead provender. Other flies represent freshwater shrimp, and so forth, but you can still do a lot of talking about trout fishing without worrying about other than the simple basic schemes.

No one can deny that knowledge of stream insects is an aid, although there are times when a trout who is stuffing himself with small mayflies is still not averse to grabbing a big grasshopper imitation. Such a fish is not "selective." That is, he is willing to take something different from the main course, and the mayfly–grasshopper switch is an extreme in "nonselectivity." Just why feeding trout are more selective at some times and locations than others is one of the things I have no explanation for. We just have to acknowledge that it's true.

Many a fisherman has been frustrated when he imitated a natural fly that kept drifting past him but could get no strikes, even though rising trout were stirring the water all around him. Perhaps they had gobbled his now-useless artificial only the day before. So he studies the situation and learns they are taking something that doesn't show up so plainly, ignoring the hatch they wanted yesterday. The preference for one natural over another cannot be explained in many cases, and we come to the lame explanation that the fish have become accustomed to taking Fly B and won't bother with Fly A. Maybe B has more nutrition, maybe it's easier to take—but in any case, this is a peak of selectivity.

Selection can take other routes. There are times when fish are strongly insistent upon a certain size of insect but seem to have little regard for its shape or color. At other times the most important thing is presentation—the way the fly floats, or drifts, in the current and the size of the leader. Taken together, these considerations seem very complex, but if you learn the basics they have a way of falling into place.

Though our interest is in fly fishing, I should mention that lures used with other than fly tackle consist mostly of spoons, spinners, plugs and weighted streamers. A spoon is generally a piece of metal which wobbles when retrieved or trolled; spinners revolve about a shaft; plugs can be made of almost anything to roughly imitate living fish or other living creatures, and may be used in conjunction with spinners. In some shapes, a weighted streamer will be called a jig. Very small spoons, spinners and plugs are sometimes cast from fly rods.

Just to complete your vocabulary, let's run down a few other fishing terms you'll be likely to encounter:

Spinning generally refers to an open reel with the line uncoiling from the spool end when the cast is made; *spin casting* is a form of spinning in which the spool is generally enclosed, the line feeding through a small opening, and its progress is generally controlled by a push button. *Bait casting* or *plug casting* employs a turning-spool reel.

Use these terms and people will know what you're talking about. The most confusing one is "bait casting," which implies that natural baits are used but usually involves artificial lures, generally a bit heavier than those cast with spinning rods.

"Feather merchant" is a kidding term for the fly fisherman, mildly derogatory when used by spin fishermen but not so when used by fly fishermen themselves.

To some anglers these words are so commonplace that they assume everyone uses them, but I'm not ashamed to define them. It's a safe bet that more than half of those who watch football don't know what a "trap play" or a "screen pass" is.

3

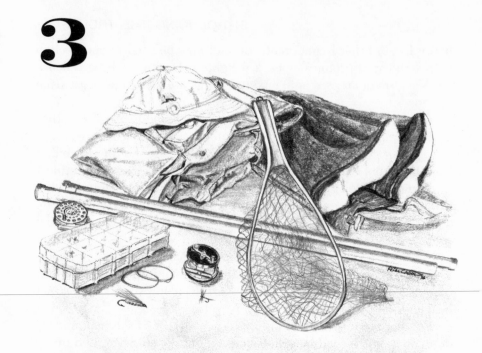

ACQUIRING THE TOOLS

You can spend a lot of time and money acquiring trout-fishing para-
phernalia before you ever wet a line, and some novices do, but it's
not really necessary. In fact, you could catch trout for a lifetime
with a single basic outfit, and I'm going to describe it and the more
useful accessories first, though afterward I'll describe second and
third outfits for special purposes that you may wish to add later.
Beyond that you're on your own, for after getting three you won't
listen to me anyway.

Your basic outfit will work on most streams as well as on lakes,
and will cover a lot of fishing. If you're completely practical, you
can wait on the other outfits until the time comes, at which point
the need will more or less jump at you. Perhaps it never will.

Studying and experimenting with tackle is fun for most fishermen even if it's not strictly necessary, but it's possible to let your check-book and desire get so far ahead of your ability that they can some-times even get in your way. And frankly, while there is no stigma to collecting tackle and most fishermen indulge in it more or less, most of us who possess a picket fence of rods and buckets of reels use only a few of them.

In choosing your first outfit you could follow the advice of an ex-pert in a good tackle shop, though if he diverges too far from what I recommend he might be something of a faddist, however fine an angler he may be. Chances are he'll be conservative, and that's what you want to begin with. But how do you find a good tackle shop?

Tackle shops aren't what they used to be for the most part—a result of the same modern marketing that has made family grocery stores scarce. The small operator can't compete unless he has some-thing unusual to offer. In most areas an entire generation of fisher-men have never loafed around a tackle shop where they knew most of the customers.

It's simple enough. Mass purchasing has made the department store a deadly competitor. And in order to compete with the depart-ment store, the big sporting-goods store has been forced to borrow some of its methods. That means things get a little impersonal, though in most cases the big sporting-goods store still has better-informed personnel than the general-department-store folks. What you're dealing with is a limited department store.

Now, in dealing with trout tackle, especially fly tackle, you may find no one in a large general department store who understands a beginner's needs, even though an expert might be able to get some-thing a little cheaper there than at a sporting-goods store. His doing that was what put the small specialized shop out of business in the first place. Many a small-tackle-shop operator has closed his door after finding a large proportion of his customers were bringing him only repair work—on gear bought at the big chain outlet.

The atmosphere of the old-time tackle shop can occasionally be found in a place that has a specialty the big store can't duplicate. For example, a fly tier might sell other equipment in an area fre-quented by trout fishermen, and a rod maker might do the same.

There is another kind of specialty tackle shop that can serve a beginner well, and I'll describe it as one that does your shopping for you. This merchant keeps to a very limited number of makes, but carries a good stock of what he does sell. Go to him for a rod and you'll generally find he's an expert—although he'll give you very little choice of brand names.

"This is the best buy in rods," he'll say, "and I stock no other makes!" Whether his tackle is superior or not, it's likely to be very good, and you take his word for it.

These days, more and more anglers buy much of their tackle by mail order, especially when they are already familiar with the general line or the particular product, and there are several well-known firms that offer excellent service to the fly fisherman and publish handsome catalogs of their wares. I still generally prefer to do my buying in person, but in situations in which this is not practical, I'd much rather order by mail from a good house than limit myself to a mediocre local source. A fairly extensive listing of dealers, tackle shops and mail-order sources appears as Appendix B at the end of this book, listed according to geographic area.

THE BASIC OUTFIT

Rods

The most important item of equipment in your basic outfit is the rod. Though some people still refer to rods by weight, I wouldn't get too involved in this, as it is much less important than the rod's action and "power." Emphasis on rod weight is a carry-over from the days when nearly all good fly rods were split bamboo and the actual heft was a guide to other characteristics.

The American Fishing Tackle Manufacturers Association has finally worked out some standards that make it easy to discuss rods. For almost a hundred years, rods and the lines that worked with them were a matter of great confusion, but they're pretty well standardized now. In fly fishing, you cast the weight of the line, and the number of the line indicates the weight and the rod that works well with it. For example, a No. 6 line goes with a No. 6 rod, and the manufacturers put the number where you can see it—generally on the rod itself, and always on the package the line comes in. The larger the number, the heavier the line and the more powerful the rod needed to accommodate it. A No. 10 line and rod would be used for truly heavy duty, as on big steelhead or salmon. For most trout fishing with both wet and dry flies I'd recommend a 5 or 6, which is a medium-to-light outfit.

Let's make our basic outfit a No. 6—easy to cast with, delicate enough for small flies and powerful enough for large trout, even in inexperienced hands. Now, this is not an "amateur" outfit, to be discarded with increased proficiency. It's a good rig for the master fisherman, and he uses it.

A good rod length is from 7½ to 8½ feet. For years fly rods became shorter and shorter, more for the appearance of delicacy than for delicacy itself. The "average" light trout rod, which used to be around 9 feet, came down to about 7 feet, and now there are even tiny wands of around 5 feet. The very short rods can be almost weightless, but they are more difficult to cast with, requiring better timing and more arm power for the longer throws. Just recently, there has been a move to a little more length again, partly because of newer materials—especially graphite, which is very light.

Some famous fishermen have attracted attention with very short rods, and most of them will admit they are handicapping themselves "for fun." For that matter, a good caster can get considerable distance by throwing a line with no rod at all, but he's doing it the hard way.

Split bamboo is the traditional material for fly rods, and it is still preferred by many trout fishermen for light operations, although they tend to go to hollow fiber glass or graphite when the line weight gets to 7 or heavier. Bamboo can be made in a wide variety of actions and has a special "feel" that appeals to many. Split-bamboo rods are made of sections glued together to make strong laminations, and the good ones are expensive because of this extensive handwork.

The first split-bamboo rods were made around 1850 and within a few years were recognized as superior tools. Their mystique was and is partly a result of the exotic material used, for the proper cane has always been difficult to secure from the Orient and only a very small part of it is usable in high-quality rods. The matching and gluing of meticulously shaped sections is a hard-learned skill, and certain rods have become collector's items because of the craftsmanship of men who combined knowledge of the material itself with a feel for the rod action to be achieved. The great bamboo-rod maker is a mechanic, a scientist and an artist, and no mass-produced glass or graphite blank, however efficient, can quite match bamboo's appeal for some sensitive (and often traditional) fishermen.

There is a special joy of possession in fine bamboo, partly because of the work that has gone into it and partly because of the revered names that appear on the rods. Of late, some old rods made by famous builders have become very expensive indeed. No two are exactly alike, of course. Some of the good ones are impregnated with materials that make them almost impervious to weather and make varnishing unnecessary.

Frankly, some of the finest bamboo rods are owned by fishermen who could do just as well with something else and are only basic casters to say the least, but they enjoy them as some duffers enjoy the finest of golf clubs.

The cheap bamboo rod was an abomination that has virtually disappeared from the scene, giving way before fiber glass. A bamboo rod that cost no more than a moderately priced glass one would be a poor investment; but you're not likely to see anything like that today. Most glass rods are pretty acceptable, and the top-grade glass apologizes to nothing. Graphite is a relatively new material, very light and with some casting characteristics of its own. It is past the experimental stage in most factories and costs about as much as bamboo. I'd say that it is definitely superior in powerful rods used for distance casting; but any of the three materials is satisfactory for a basic outfit, and glass is least expensive.

A good fly rod will work for dry flies, wet flies, streamers and nymphs. For years there was much talk of the "dry-fly action," which was a little "faster" than that used for wet flies. In other words, the rod was a little stiffer for its weight and recoiled more quickly after being bent. But now nearly all rods are a bit faster than the ancient bamboos.

Some fishermen are insistent upon slow-bending rods that bend "clear down into the butt" on every cast, utilizing the entire rod length. Others bend more progressively, letting most of the cast come from the tip section. Extremes should be avoided to begin with, and an over-the-counter No. 6 will probably be moderate.

Someone who has been casting for some time may develop a

liking for especially soft or especially stiff rods, but he shouldn't trust his own judgment at first. If there is such a thing as an "average" rod, that's what he should have.

The human element enters into rod and line weight. Get a 6 line for your 6 rod and it will work fine, but there are some fishermen who eventually decide they prefer a 5 or 7 line for a 6 rod. Don't let that confuse you, because it is a technical matter that doesn't mean anything for a long while. Besides, some of it is imagination. Using a heavier line than what is recommended for a rod is called "overloading" it, and it happens that I like a slightly overloaded rod; however, some better casters than I am go the other way. Avoid this nitpicking at the outset.

If a line is too heavy, the casting motion must become very slow, for the burdened rod straightens slowly. If the line is too light, the caster must swish the rod faster to keep the line from falling to the ground or water before he makes the cast. But that's enough about casting for now.

Reels

Single-action fly reels are almost universal on light and medium fly rods used by veteran fishermen. They're a bit snobbish about this, for the fact is that an automatic reel is excellent for light fishing. The automatic takes up loose line with a spring. Its only real disadvantages are that it is rather heavy, and that it doesn't work on fish that make long runs when hooked, since it wasn't built to give out a great deal of line under pressure.

The accepted light single-action reels are made of alloys, graphite or plastic, and for the basic trout rod they are pretty small in size and capacity. Single action means that when you turn the handle once the spool goes around once—pretty obvious, since the handle is usually fastened directly to the spool. A multiplying reel, often used for heavier fishing, is geared to wind faster than you turn the handle.

It's stylish to use a very small fly reel on a rod of the class we're discussing. It looks dainty, it's light and it takes up little room, but I don't like the very smallest ones for two reasons. One is that the spool is so small in diameter, even when full, that the fly line is necessarily stored in small loops and doesn't want to straighten out

Some typical fly reels. At lower right is an ultralight made largely of graphite. Just above it is an automatic, and the reel at top right is a multiplier.

well when it's pulled off for casting (that's "stripping" line). The other obvious shortcoming is that you must turn the spool a great deal to take up your line, which is a nuisance when you're in a hurry.

Too much has been made of "balancing" a fly reel to a rod. If you want to get technical, the ideal balance would be with a reel heavy enough so that the rod would not tip one way or the other when you held it horizontally with your hand open beneath the grip. With a heavy rod, that would have some advantage, but with our light No. 6 it would be all right for the rod tip to overbalance the reel, and there are some casters who say they can't feel the rod's action properly unless the outfit is a little top-heavy. I don't think it's important one way or the other.

Some of the most rugged and durable fly reels are very modestly priced and made in America, but there are fishermen who insist upon costly English reels of fine workmanship. The expensive ones are more delicate in many cases, are easily bent and may have such small tolerances that a little dirt can foul them up. Nevertheless, the workmanship is there, and there's joy and prestige in ownership.

You don't need much of a drag (the part that brakes the reel to keep it from turning too freely when you're stripping line or playing a fish) for most trout fishing. Most fly reels have a click, and some of the finest have noisy clicks that scream when a fish runs and do the same thing when you yank off line while casting. They can get too loud to suit me, but it's a matter of personal taste. When you have a fish on, a little click noise can help because you can tell without looking when a fish is taking line. It is good to have an easily removable spool for cleaning, and spare spools are convenient if you carry more than one type of line.

Lines

There are three common shapes of line for stream trout fishing. For most use, the double-tapered line is best. It has a long middle section that's of uniform diameter and it tapers down to smaller diameter at both ends. The taper at the fishing end makes it possible to lay a small fly down more gently, and the line can be reversed when it begins to wear, giving you two lines for the purchase of one. The level line is of the same diameter all the way, is inexpensive and casts just as well as the double-taper, but can't be used so delicately. The weight-forward, or "torpedo," line is made up of a short, heavy forward section with a little taper in front and with the back part of small, uniform diameter. It's for distance instead of delicacy, and don't worry about it until you see a need. Maybe you never will.

There is another specialized form of line for extreme distance—a short "shooting head" of heavy line attached to very small running line, often of monofilament, which is bought separately. For most purposes your line should float on top of the water. For special uses there are lines that sink fast, sink slowly or have sinking tips with the rest of the line floating. But since we're talking first about our basic, general-purpose outfit, you only need one line to start with—a double-tapered, floating No. 6. You can add the others as you encounter the need for them.

Leaders

Since even the lightest fly lines are still relatively coarse, a long segment of tapered material—almost always monofilament nylon these days—is interpolated between the line and the fly. "Leader," as such material is called, can be bought in a variety of weights and lengths, and comes in either knotted or knotless form, the former being preferred by most anglers. Even though you buy all the rest of your equipment, including flies, I think you'll eventually prefer to tie your own leaders—a practice that's avoided by most beginning anglers and a few veterans. It's one of those things that look a little complicated at first glance, and it doesn't appear very exciting. Perhaps exciting is something it never becomes, but it's so easy, and so far the best solution, that you'll find it discussed in some detail later on in Chapter 7.

Leaders are generally classified by X rating rather than pound test, because the caster is more interested in diameter than in strength. X sizes range from the experts' 7X (.004 inch) up to the relatively massive 0X (.011 inch). To start off, I'd buy a couple of 9- or 10-foot, knotted leaders in 4X, which will run from 3 to 4 pounds in test. After you've tied a few new tippets (fine terminal ends) on these, you can start tying your own.

Flies

Collections of flies tend to sneak up on you, and after several seasons you can have a big investment in a single box without realizing it. Almost every trout fisherman has lost boxes of flies without recalling their value until he does a bit of figuring. A friend of mine grumbled routinely about losing a small, well-filled box of salmon flies, but it was several days before he estimated they had cost him $250 through the years. Checking your boxes from time to time can prevent you from carrying too many flies you won't use and might lose.

Twenty dollars' worth of flies can give you a season's fishing or more, but most of us add to our supplies almost constantly. Your very first flies can be selected by the dealer and will probably be chosen for the area in which he operates. For starters you might have about a dozen dry flies in sizes from 10 to 16. About half of them could be highly visible ones and the rest of duller shades. Then you should have three or four nymphs of assorted sizes, a couple of small streamers and two or three wet flies of about Size 10 or 12.

Go easy until you know exactly where you'll be fishing. Almost invariably you'll find you don't trust your first purchases and will begin fishing with other patterns proved at the scene by other fishermen.

The Working Knots

Once you have your line, leaders and flies, you need some means of attaching them to each other, and this, again, can be as simple or as complicated as you want to make it. Knots in themselves are interesting, and I know wonderful fishermen who can tie them by the dozens, but if you can make and/or tie new tippets onto your leader, tie your leader to your line at one end and to the fly at the other and splice backing to your fly line, you can get by very nicely for a lifetime. A total of three knots will serve these purposes, though some fishermen never learn even that many.

The three essential knots are (1) the improved clinch, for fastening the fly to the leader; (2) the blood, or barrel, knot, for attaching

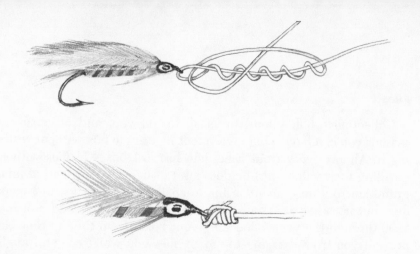

The three indispensable angler's knots: above, the improved clinch, used for typing on your flies; below, the blood knot, for typing new tippets onto the leader; at right, the nail knot, for attaching the leader to the line.

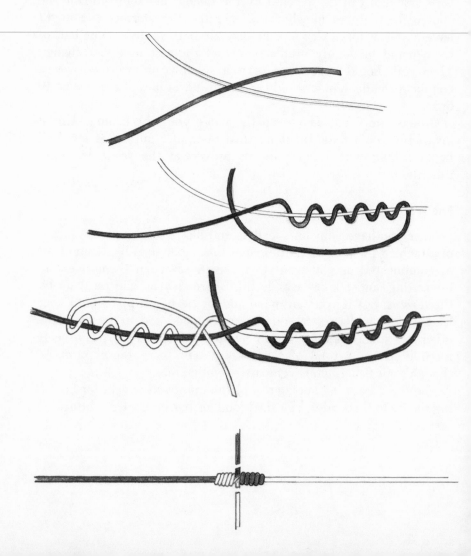

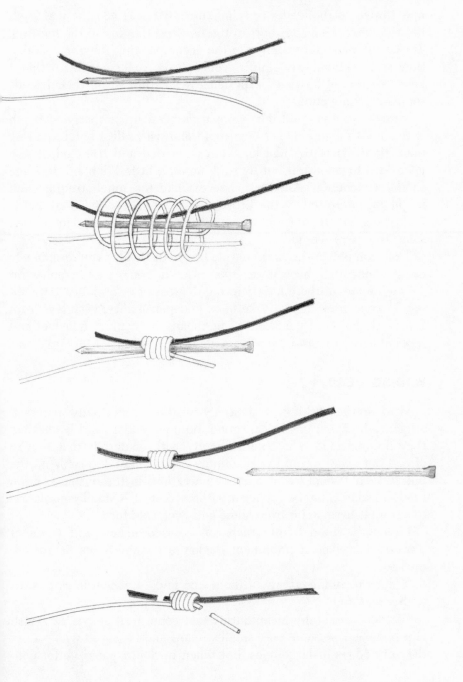

new tippets to the leader or tying your own, and (3) the nail knot, for attaching the leader butt to the line and the line to the backing. These three knots are shown in the accompanying diagrams, and if they seem ridiculously simple, you may be shaken to learn that I know anglers of 20 years' experience who still call on their friends for leader connections.

Most knots that pull out weren't snugged up properly to begin with, and it's a good idea to moisten them with saliva before pulling them tight. After the nail knot has been tied and trimmed, it is a good idea to smooth it out by rubbing on a little Pliobond, or some similar concoction. And if this seems like too much trouble, you might be interested in the little patented Leader Link that Eagle Claw puts out. It's not quite an invisible splice, but it's closer than some knot tiers ever get.

That completes the *basic* outfit; but realistically, you're going to need some other accessories too, even if you're not a collector. Though many of these have varying degrees of essentiality, depending on your area, taste, pocketbook and personality, very few trout fishermen can get by without some means of keeping their feet and legs (at least) dry and, even more important, warm.

WADING GEAR

Most stream fishing is done by wading, and many practical anglers who fish a great deal spend more on waders and boots than they do on tackle. The chief difficulty with waders is that they're often not waterproof—a seemingly fundamental problem the builders can't seem to solve after generations in the business. Even though leakers may be replaced without cost, it is small consolation to a trout fisherman far from home with wet, cold feet.

I recently stood before racks of assorted makes and types of waders and asked a prominent dealer just which ones he recommended.

"I don't recommend any of them," he said. "But you have to start with *something*."

"Waders" generally mean outfits that come well above the waist. Hip boots will serve in very small streams and for those who stay in the very edges of large ones, but when in doubt you'd better consider waders, and you'll probably end up with both. In recent years the price of waders has had little bearing on their ability to repel cold water, and when you get new ones, your first move should be to put them on and sit down in a well-filled bathtub, preferably using lukewarm water. This undignified procedure results in some tense moments and occasionally in a sense of outrage. Apparently the builders have worked out no good way of testing their product—an unusual situation in a nation with representatives strolling across the moon. A collection of the furious letters written to manufacturers and dealers concerning waders would make an interesting volume.

Chest waders should be long, coming well up under the arms and suspended by husky galluses. A belt around the middle reduces the silhouette exposed to pushing current and will keep out a remarkable amount of water in case of an upset—something that will occur eventually.

Waders must be divided into two classes—stocking-foot and boot-foot. Stocking-foot waders are used with separate wading shoes, which may be ordinary tennis footwear if the bottom is not slippery, but which must be highly specialized if the bottom is slick. Stocking waders can be very inexpensive in the light plastic form, but these probably won't be very durable. You can carry spares— but usually you discover failure by getting wet. Light plastic snags easily, but can be patched quickly. Stocking waders are light in weight and generally better than boot-foot waders for walking long distances. The most expensive stocking waders are made of fabric.

The disadvantages of stocking waders are that it takes considerable time to put them on and take them off, and that after they and the shoes that go with them get wet, they are a messy bundle. You should always wear heavy socks between the waders and the wading shoes to avoid chafing, making a total of five items to misplace in the back of the car; and once everything gets wet—well, everything is wet.

Boot-foot waders are easy to put on and take off, but a nuisance to dry out. There are electrical units that can be slipped down into them for that purpose, and it's wise to suspend them upside down for airing between trips. A large percentage of trout fishermen who use boot-foot waders prefer those made of fabric. The heavy-duty

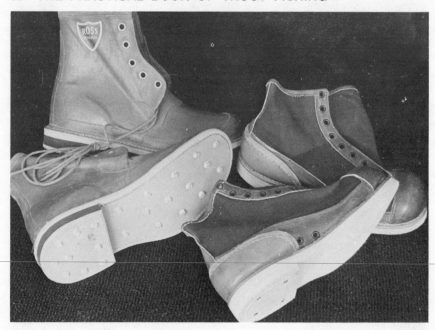

Wading shoes for use with stocking-foot waders. Rubber shoes at left have soft metal studs. Canvas-and-leather shoes at right have felt soles.

industrial waders with a rubber exterior are most durable and have the best record regarding leaks, but they are heavy and seldom available with nonslip soles. Nevertheless, many fishermen who spend much time in the water use them, attaching some sort of sandals or special soles for traction. Such an outfit is really tiring when you're walking on dry ground, though weight doesn't hurt and may even be a help when you're in deep water. Black waders can be surprisingly hot when exposed to the sun.

Get waders large enough that you can wear two pairs of heavy socks under them. In cold water you may want to wear insulated underwear under the socks, and some fishermen use oversized, down-filled underwear *over* their regular clothing and under the waders. Condensation can be a nuisance, and many "sweating" waders are brought back to the dealer in the belief they're leaking when they're not. I know one dealer who supplies his friends with reduced-cost waders that have been returned with persistent accusations of leakage. If the complaining fisherman is a good customer, he just replaces them without argument, even if tests show condensation is the culprit.

Wader legs should be long enough to let your knees bend fully, for closely fitted ones can immobilize you—or split. Waders are seldom flattering to anyone's figure, and have probably done much to drive women away from the whole fishing project.

There is no rubber tread that works on really slippery bottoms, and really slick stones must be felt to be appreciated. A stream can get slippery because of growth on the rocks, often invisible to a casual observer, and because of water polishing. A fall in knee-deep water can get you wet, and a fall in waist-deep water might even

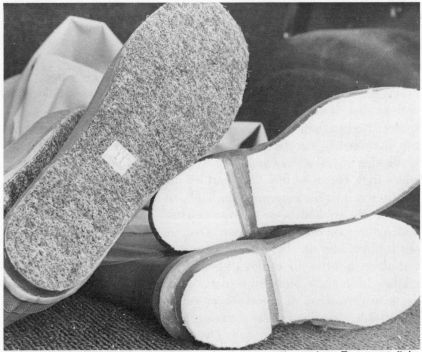

Carpeting (left) and felt are old standards on wader soles. For most fishing they are hard to beat, despite fairly rapid wear.

take you downstream for a piece, but a fall in 2 inches of water can injure you seriously. So there must be something special on your soles.

Felt shoes, which are expensive, are available on boot-foot waders, wading sandals or shoes, and they work very well in most cases. They can also be had on fabric hip-length boots, or "hippers." Of late, soles made of nylon carpeting have been used to serve the same purpose, and they often wear longer. It's hard to tell how a felt or carpet sole will wear by looking at it, and evidently people in the business are mystified too, for some soles last well and some don't. In some areas where there's a great deal of trout fishing you can get replacement soles installed at shoe-repair shops. Sometimes they're better than the originals, and sometimes they aren't as good.

Felt or carpet works in most waters, but there are better things when the bottom feels like lumps of greased ice. Most other materials are bulky and somewhat awkward, especially for walking on dry ground.

Studs or plates of soft alloy have remarkable gripping power, better than those of harder steel or iron unless the latter appears in very sharp spikes. These metal rigs can be had in wading shoes to go over stocking-foot waders or in sandals to go over boot-foot waders with rubber or felt soles. Many fishermen have had aluminum golf spikes fitted to their wader soles, but they're pretty long and easy to trip over unless carefully trimmed off. I have used sandals with small, sharp steel spikes and they were fine until they wore smooth, when they began to feel like marbles underfoot. It's a lot of work, but they can be filed sharp again. Hobs of soft iron were once popular but are seldom seen anymore. There are also chain sandals, which are good on some bottoms. Overall, though, I think your best bet for standing on slick rocks in swift water is aluminum or other soft alloy, and the plates don't need to be sharp. So far, the best for me has been some aluminum plates fastened to some buffed-down dress rubbers that fit tightly over my rubber wader soles, and I understand that one firm is planning to manufacture them in quantity. Almost every year brings a new gadget.

Wading staffs, some of them collapsible, are carried by many operators in swift water, and almost all waders pick up streamside

Unusual nonslip gear for waders. At left are small steel spikes. At right are aluminum cleats attached to a pullover rubber that fits over ordinary boot or wader foot. The combination at right is of recent design and is proving highly successful in heavy, slippery water. (Courtesy Dan Bailey's Fly Shop)

sticks occasionally for help over bad spots. You may think that I am overemphasizing all of this wading business, but it can become a major element of a fishing trip. You will find some suggestions on your own wading techniques later on in Chapter 7.

OTHER ACCESSORIES

You should get a vest, and right away. Nothing else can keep your innumerable gadgets so well organized, and most regular fishermen leave theirs loaded the year around. Through the seasons some vests acquire things even their owners no longer recognize, and they are likely to take on a patina that makes old fishing hats appear almost sterile. Vests are made short, to keep your enclosed treasures out of the water, and some of them are ultrashort for deep wading. Best described as a bundle of pockets strategically stitched together, the vest should have good closures on all compartments and a variety of pocket sizes.

Of late I have found some vests that actually have too many pockets for me, for I have to do a bit of hunting for emergency items now and then. This is the first public record of that complaint, I am sure, since fishermen have continually clamored for more pockets.

A practical form of fishing vest, modeled by Fred Terwilliger. Pockets must have closures on them. Snaps are fairly handy, but these days many anglers are turning to Velcro fastenings.

Anyway, you need plenty of them, but if you don't clean them out every year or two you'll end up with a backbreaking burden.

There should be a large back pocket for rain gear, lunch and other bulky items such as spare reels, while most of the flies or lures will go in the front pockets, filed away in plastic or metal boxes and "books." I'll describe some of the other essentials that go into a vest, and you'll eventually collect a lot more, most of which you'll never use.

Remember that once you have your waders cinched in and your vest on over them, your pants pockets are available only with considerable contortion, and some items must be either duplicated or transferred when you suit up.

Despite the claims that modern fly lines never need dressing, or even much cleaning, you'll be happy to find a jar or tin of line dressing handy, and nearly all fly fishermen carry it in a front pocket. Much of it is applied to lines, but as time goes by it also tends to get smeared over the vest, and the greasy splotches identify you as a fisherman who has been around. Before modern lines were developed, it was necessary to dress the old silk lines frequently if they were to float. The new lines need it less but will still float better if you use it occasionally, and a high-floating line helps in much of your fishing as well as your casting.

Solutions to make your dry flies float better come in small spray cans, bottles or jars. For small flies, liquid is easier to apply than paste, and it has less tendency to mat the hackles. Some fishermen use their line dressing for their flies, and although it may not be dainty, it's efficient. As far as I know, there's no bad commercial line dressing and no bad fly dope.

You'll need a little piece of inner tube or other rubber to pull your leaders through to keep them from curling up. You can buy a leader straightener with a hole for a cord to attach to your vest, or you can cut several pieces of inner tube and lose them one at a time.

There are some solutions for the purpose of making leaders and wet flies sink readily, but many fishermen never use them at all.

A little spring-reel device such as is used for keys can be pinned to your vest and is very handy for holding fingernail clippers for trimming leaders and, occasionally, flies. Folding scissors are good too

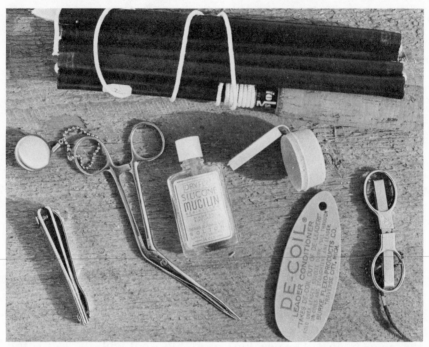

Handy contents of a fishing vest. Top, collapsible wading staff. Below, left to right: Nail clippers, forceps on spring retractor, dry-fly dope, line dressing, leader straightener and folding scissors.

and it's a matter of personal preference, but either is handier than a pocketknife.

You'll probably want a knife of some kind, though, and if it has a hook disgorger you can use that frequently. Perhaps even better, however, are the small forceps available for that purpose, preferably attached by a cord or to one of the little retracting spools. Tools are usually better than fingers when a fish is to be released.

Eventually you'll need several little spools of monofilament leader material of different sizes to replace tippets with, and some vests have special pockets for them. If you prefer, you can just string them on a heavy cord in order of their size and tie the ends of the cord together.

Landing nets are used by a sizable number of trout fishermen. Some come supplied with elastic cords that you simply put over your head and under one arm, but when the net catches in the brush and then pulls loose it can deliver a stiff punch, probably at the base of your ear. It's better to use what's known as a French snap attached to the vest just back of your neck. It can be released with one hand and keeps the net out of the way when it isn't in use. There are also folding nets which can be stored inside a large pocket. You might also want a tape measure and some pocket scales, and possibly a small flashlight.

You'll surely want a patching kit for your waders, insect dope and something to keep your lips from chapping. A miniature first-aid kit is worthwhile, and you may wish to include sun lotion.

Most vests come with a little sheepskin patch for carrying flies that have been used and are too wet to put back into the box. If the vest doesn't have it, you can buy a little patch of sheepskin on a safety pin. This has some advantage, since it can be easily replaced if it wears out, and a permanently attached pad complicates the laundering job when you finally become ashamed of your vest.

The picturesque wicker creels of the past have almost disappeared from the scene. They were bulky and hard to clean, and after a few years of use they could be smelled for a considerable distance. A cheaper and more convenient means of carrying fish these days is in a canvas creel.

Containers for the larger flies are no problem. They can be kept in heavy plastic boxes with hinged lids, compartmented for convenience, and if the boxes are transparent it's easy to find what you want. Other efficient boxes have grooves to hold the hooks, and some grip the hooks in little coil springs. There is a variety of metal hook clips that work well inside boxes. Generally, it's more convenient to use several boxes, each containing a type of fly or streamer. Large streamers can be carried in leather or soft-plastic books, pressed in sheepskin or similar material. "Hardware" lures are usually kept in plastic boxes.

A sheepskin hatband is good for large flies and streamers, but I think you'll be happier if you reserve it for the flies you're using constantly, with more permanent storage confined to boxes and books.

Very small flies, especially dries, are not so simple, and the wind has robbed me of more tiny flies than the fish have gotten away

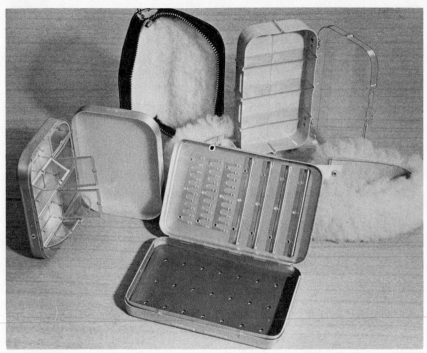

Fly containers. Box with transparent lids on compartments is at left. Zipper "book" and simple compartmented box at top. Box with hook clips leans against fleece hatband.

with. Putting too many of them loose in one compartment of a box is dangerous; one gust of wind can leave you staring at an empty container or floundering frantically after them as they bounce downstream. There are some well-made aluminum boxes with small lidded compartments, the transparent lids spring-loaded and held by tiny catches. I use that kind, but the catches require constant attention, and if they get bent a little they'll open at the wrong time, usually in a high wind.

Some fishermen keep their very small flies stuck into thin sheets of foam rubber fitted into aluminum or plastic boxes. This is a safe method, but the foam comes apart with use and must be replaced frequently.

BIGGER AND SMALLER

I've talked mainly about a basic trout outfit, although most of the facts apply equally to heavy-duty and ultralight equipment. Now let's go into rather specialized rods and lines.

Our basic outfit is a little light for throwing big streamers for long distances on wide rivers, and there's a little paradox where rod power is concerned. If you try to make long casts with large flies and a light rod, you find that it's much more work than using a heavier outfit. You're using it for something it wasn't intended for, and you've lost the ease of operation for which you got the lighter outfit.

This is a simple matter that's widely misunderstood. For example, a very small woman angler is often hard to sell on anything but the lightest rods. The very small rod feels good, and for short distances with light flies casting is effortless, so the lady doesn't want it out of her hands. When she goes to a situation where her casts must be longer and her flies must be large and wind-resistant, she still wants to take her little rod with her. The fact is that a more powerful rod would be less work under the new conditions. I am not saying that an 80-pound girl is likely to be happy with a giant salmon rod taking a No. 11 line, but she needs more power for a big streamer and a wide river than she does for a placid brook. An overworked rod takes effort.

Heavy-Duty

For heavy duty, a rod taking a No. 8 or No. 9 line will suit most of us and is powerful enough to handle any trout or salmon. A length of 8½ feet is about right. Some of the graphite rods are so light in weight that they are popular in greater lengths. At about this point the bamboo rod begins to lose its popularity, as a bamboo taking an 8 line begins to be a bit heavy to handle as compared with glass or graphite. Most of the long-range power casters have abandoned it.

Once casting proficiency has been developed, almost any adult can handle a No. 8 outfit for considerable periods of time, and I have watched many slight women do so. However, when we get to No. 10 rods and lines, it takes pretty good timing and a fairly well-conditioned arm to fish all day. My wife, who weighs about 110 pounds and is an experienced caster, prefers a No. 8 rod for her heavy trout or salmon fishing. She can cast very well with a No. 10 for a couple of hours, but gets too tired in an all-day session.

The heavy-duty outfit requires a large-capacity reel with considerable backing. Here an automatic is a bad choice, and if you prefer a multiplying (geared) reel there is no objection. However, the majority of expert fishermen use single-action reels. For this outfit you need a reasonably good drag, although a great deal of adjustment is unnecessary. When a fish runs against a fly reel, the rod is generally bent so much that the effective drag tension is greatly magnified by line pulling through the guides.

I am not down-rating the fine heavy-duty reels used in both fresh and salt water, and if you spend a great deal of time with very large fish they could be an excellent investment. They cost about as much as a fine rod, but will last a lifetime with reasonable care.

Now to the other extreme—the tiny rod for the most delicate fishing. Frankly, the basic No. 6 outfit will do this job pretty well and will be superior in many instances, so I am not really pushing for the ultralight. You can get by very nicely without it; but you fish for fun, and if it's added pleasure, go to it.

Ultralight

Most ultralight fly outfits include rods of 7 feet or less, but they can be had with longer sticks and still be light enough to suit almost anyone. A No. 3 line is about right, and you can use a peewee reel if you want to, although the one that works on your No. 6 rod will serve. About the only excuse for a tiny reel is the appearance of delicacy.

How short a rod? Well, I have used a 6½-footer a great deal on small streams and never cared for anything much shorter, but you can get it down to toy class if you want to. It is harder to fish with very short rods for several reasons, but if you consider them the mark of the master, so be it. I might as well say right here that fishermen work on their images more than they admit, and a deliberate handicap is an important element in most sport fishing anyway.

You don't have to worry about the quality of hardware on most trout rods, but the construction of reel seats has driven me into occasional apoplectic tantrums. The offender is usually part of a very light rod where to save weight and give the impression of delicacy the reel is held on with only a pair of slip rings instead of a full reel seat. Using these doodads I have dropped reels into cold, swift water from Patagonia to Alaska, generally with a desirable trout on the other end of the line. I admit that if the reel's plate is

Swift mountain stream in the East where a short rod is an advantage. The caster looks over his shoulder before each cast, fitting his line between obstacles.

shaped just right and the rings are just so, the thing will work, but some combinations become a sort of ejection unit. If you can get it, use a reel seat with firm screw-on fastenings, unless you don't mind use of a little adhesive tape.

RODS IN GENERAL

Now that we've looked at three outfits, some general observations about rods won't hurt. I'd say anything less than 7½ feet is a short rod. Anything more than 8½ feet in a trout rod is long. A 10-footer is an extreme, and so is a 6-footer.

A long rod carries the line up high during casting—a decided advantage, since one of the most common casting faults is letting the line strike the ground or water in back of the angler at the wrong time. The longer rod is especially helpful when you're wading deep. A longer rod is more forgiving of mistakes made by the fisherman; for example, if he jerks too hard in setting the hook, the jerk is somewhat softened by the rod length. A longer rod also holds more line off the water when the fly is being fished—an advantage in some delicate situations—and it picks up line more easily before a cast.

On the other hand, the long rod isn't nearly so handy to carry in brushy areas, and its leverage puts more strain on the fisherman's hand and arm, regardless of the rod's weight. You may be able to set a hook quicker with a short rod, and you may be able to cast better under low trees. It may also be easier to keep your line down out of some high winds. With the short rod you have more leverage on the fish with the rod pointed straight up, but by pointing the tip somewhat downward you can duplicate that effect with a longer stick. On some brushy streams the long rod may keep the casting line clear up out of trouble.

The cork handles come in various shapes. Most factory ones are round, but some fishermen prefer customized grips to fit their hands, and some like a flattened place for the thumb on the forward part of the handle. One of the best grips I've used was a customized "hammer handle," oblong in cross section, but I haven't seen any really bad rod grips lately. With a fairly heavy stick, you need enough cork to get a firm grip. Otherwise, don't worry about it.

Most of the better fiber-glass rods have ferrules (the connections for rod sections) made of the same material—not nearly so likely to stick as metal ones. The good bamboo rods have carefully fitted metal ferrules, but you should use care with them, as a little corrosion can cause sticking. None of the graphite rods I've seen had metal ferrules. Ferrules give more trouble than the rest of the rod. They can come loose, they can freeze and they can split. Many fishermen lubricate metal ferrules slightly by rubbing them against their noses, and this is better than nothing.

The majority of fly rods today are made in two sections, and many bamboo models have two tips, one of them a spare in case of breakage. Since ferrules, in theory, change the rod action by adding a little stiffness in most cases, multisectioned rods do not have a reputation for casting quite as well as those with only two pieces, but modern design has pretty well whipped this objection. A "suitcase" or "pack" rod comes apart in several sections, so that it takes up little room, and I was completely fooled recently when I was handed a glass one that looked like a one-piecer and cast like one too, as nearly as I could tell; then its designer broke it down into five sections. The fewer the ferrules the better where durability is concerned, but I wouldn't worry about casting qualities. Rod design has come a long way.

Wire "snake" guides are generally used to keep the overall weight down, but the tip guide and the one nearest the reel (the "stripping" guide) are often made of something bulkier, since the line enters them at a sharp angle and wire would cause too much resistance and wear.

Some light glass rods have deceptively large diameter near the butt, a matter of gaining stiffness with thin walls. Graphite rods are smaller in diameter because of the greater stiffness of the material itself. Some high-grade bamboo rods are hollow near the butt and appear rather beefy there.

Rod cases, or "tubes," for the more expensive models are generally made of aluminum or plastic, and the rod itself is usually protected from abrasion by a cloth or plastic bag inside the tube. Budget-priced rods often come in cardboard tubes, which afford only temporary protection as issued but can be toughened up by application of waterproof tape on the exterior. Sections of plastic plumber's conduit can be cut into very rugged rod cases at little cost, and you can get fitted caps for them.

Air, train or bus travel requires a little special attention for rods. Some fishermen carrying several in aluminum tubes simply tape them together, with the feeling that in unity there is strength. Although this has worked for years for others, my own rods have occasionally been accepted as a challenge by muscular baggage handlers, and I've had some smashed and bent aluminum tubes. There are large and heavy aluminum or plastic tubes which take several rods in their cloth bags, and although they're not exactly cheap, most of them seem to be pretty tough.

I vote my rods as being the baggage most likely to be lost, and some of them are much more widely traveled than I am. The explanation is simple: fly-rod cases are just a bit too long to fit neatly with other luggage and often end up in a separate section of the baggage compartment, thus finding their way to exotic destinations. Keep your rods with you if you can, and if you can't do that, check their welfare at every opportunity. It may be that my personal guardian angel is lax about them, but I once had them temporarily lost on three out of five successive airline trips.

SPINNING TACKLE

Spinning tackle for trout is much simpler than fly gear. Start with a rod capable of handling lures as light as ⅛ ounce, and you should be able to use things that weigh up to somewhat more than ¼ ounce without difficulty. The rod can be of almost any length, and there are some handy little ones of about 5 feet. Most trout fishing is handled best with 4- or 6-pound-test monofilament line. The smaller open-faced reels are most efficient of all, although requiring a bit more expertise than closed-face, or "push-button," reels. The closed-face reels run the line through a cone, look like modernistic pencil sharpeners and are a bit complicated in construction. They require more care than open-faced reels, but are the easiest of all for a beginner to cast with.

There's a highly skilled form of spin fishing for trout that employs light or medium spinning tackle and regular trout flies with a "bubble" type of floating weight—similar to bobber fishing at first glance, but capable in expert hands of delivering flies to small targets with considerable delicacy. Some spin fishermen cast short sections of heavy material which resemble regular fly lines.

The beginner's most common error in stream spinning for trout is the use of line that's too heavy and loses him distance, accuracy and delicacy. For most stream fishing, 6-pound line is plenty, and in smaller creeks there'll be more fish and more fun with 4-pound or lighter. Spin fishing for large steelhead or salmon is a different ball game entirely, and the outfits used for them are about the same as those chosen for light saltwater fishing.

Light spinning gear and small spinners took these silver salmon (cohos) from a small Alaska creek. The coho, partly because of its migratory habits, can behave very differently in various parts of its range.

BAIT CASTING

Bait-casting tackle is efficient for lures weighing more than ¼ ounce and isn't employed as much as it might be. The fact is that fishermen who take the trouble to learn bait casting are likely to become fly fishermen as well and use the latter method for most of their trout fishing.

One of the most effective forms of steelhead fishing employs a long, soft-tipped casting rod, generally two-handed, and a free-spooling reel (the handle doesn't turn as the spool pays out the casting line). Although this rig is excellent for conventional spoons, weighted spinners and plugs, it is frequently used with drifted lures that bounce along the bottom attached to "pencil" sinkers, cut to match the current. This began with the Cherry Bobber, which imitates salmon eggs, a popular steelhead food, but there are other lures of many colors and shapes that work about the same way.

Though purists may frown on it, ordinary black bass bait-casting tackle is excellent for much trout and salmon fishing. This coho was taken with a spoon in brackish coastal water before beginning its upstream journey for spawning.

EQUIPMENT CHECKLIST

Basic Choice

Rod taking No. 6 line (7½' to 8½')
Double-taper floating line to match
Light single-action reel
*Several 9' leaders, 4X
Assorted flies—dries, wets, nymphs and streamers in boxes or books

Optional Extras

Spare reel or spool with double-taper sinking line
Spare reel or spool with sinking-tip line

Heavy-Duty Outfit

Rod taking No. 8 line (8½' to 9')
Weight-forward floating line to match
Large capacity single-action (or multiplying) reel
*Several 9' leaders, 0X
Assorted large streamers

Optional Extras

Spare reel or spool with weight-forward sinking line
Spare reel or spool with shooting head and backing

Ultralight Outfit

Rod taking No. 3 line (6½' to 7½')
Double-taper floating line to match
Ultralight reel
*Several 12' leaders, 6X
Assorted small dry flies

Optional Equipment

Small first-aid kit, small flashlight, suntan lotion, small screwdriver, metal plates for waders, stream thermometer, wading staff, hook file or hone, compact binoculars, photographic equipment

Vest Contents

Clippers on spring reel, forceps, line dressing or cleaner, dry-fly dressing, lead strips for weighting sinking flies and nymphs, tippet materials, rubber tab for straightening leaders, insect repellent, repair kit for waders, assorted fly boxes and books

Clothing and Auxiliary Gear

Fishing vest, waders with cleated or felt soles, suspenders and belt for above, hip boots, canvas creel, landing net, heavy socks, hat or cap, lightweight rain jacket, knife suitable for cleaning fish, polarized sunglasses, complete set of dry clothes

* If you tie your own leaders, which I recommend, you will need an assortment of leader materials instead, ranging from 30-pound-test to 6X.

4

USING THE TOOLS

There's a lot more to trout fishing than fly casting, but you still must learn to cast if you are going to fish for trout with flies, and you may as well do it right. Some veteran fishermen never bothered about that part until they had to unlearn some bad habits, and some new anglers never became veterans because the whole thing seemed like too much trouble. There's no excuse for either.

Fly casting in itself is a game, sometimes competitive, and there are real casters on most streams today. I say "real casters" because until recent years, fly casting for most fishermen was simply a matter of getting a fly into the water. A few years back, you could draw gasps and cheers from a sportsmen's-show audience by throwing a fly 80 feet. Today, most experienced fishermen would yawn at such an exhibition. Nevertheless, a great many otherwise proficient anglers are needlessly handicapped by their casting.

Casting ability is too often rated by the distance someone can throw a line, which is natural in that it is something which can be measured. But the ability to throw a long line is primarily an indication that a shorter cast can be made without undue effort, and undue effort is what we're trying to avoid. Beginning fly fishermen are most likely to give it up when it becomes hard work. They either quit fly fishing or confine their efforts to "flop casting," in which an expensive rod is used as if it were a cane pole. You can catch a lot of trout flop-casting, but you're missing much of the fun of fishing.

Fly casting becomes progressively easier for a long time for most of us. As we go along we learn little tricks of timing we don't even recognize ourselves and which can't be easily described. For casting, if it's properly done, isn't hard work. The most lamented dropouts in the fly-casting business are those who learn to throw a good line but are just enough off in their timing that it is too much effort and they

Fly-fishing students watch instructor Don Williams of the Orvis school demonstrate roll casting.

quit, feeling they've learned all there is to know but still having a sore arm. In addition to being a little off in their timing, they've been trying too hard.

Having labored through several thousands of pages of advice about fly casting, I'm convinced that a rather simple subject has been beaten to death with typewriters, and many otherwise competent instructors are confusing their readers with catch phrases and gimmicky tricks billed as breakthroughs in technique. A book or article on fly fishing, in order to sell, needs a new slant, a new approach or a new "system." All of the methods end up pretty much the same in the end. It isn't that too much is being written—simply that all those pages should be devoted to simplification instead of scheming.

Of course, the best way to simplify casting for the novice is *show* him what to do, and fancy explanations usually don't make much sense before you have *felt* what they are talking about. Fortunately, casting clinics are readily accessible in most areas these days, and many veteran anglers are also only too happy to help a beginner get started, so it shouldn't be too difficult to get someone to provide a personal demonstration of the matters I'm about to discuss. If you're really stuck, especially with respect to some of the fancier casts, let me recommend a remarkable graphic treatment of the subject: *Fly Fishing with Lefty Kreh* (Lippincott), which features Irv Swope's exceptional sequence photographs. Swope's pictures, for once, carry all the clarity of diagrams, and if you think a picture treatment might help you, I'd try Lefty's book first. But now, let's talk about basic principles.

The first thing to understand is that in casting a fly you are throwing the weight of the line instead of the weight of a lure. You pick it up from the water with the rod tip, throw it back over your shoulder and then lay it back on the water again. You are throwing what we'll call a "loop," although it is really a long "U" since it's open at one end. It is almost exactly the motion used in operating a long bullwhip, except that the rod helps. (Perhaps that's not very explanatory in these days in which there are more fly casters than bullwhippers, but one of the true naturals I've encountered in fly casting was formerly an outfitter and horse packer who handled a string of mules with a blacksnake whip.)

This loop we're talking about is formed as the line goes back over your shoulder. It's something that can be seen as well as felt, and there is no law against watching it take shape, although some new casters seem afraid to look back. When you can form that loop with your line about the same every time, you are already a fly caster, and everything you learn from then on deals with the loop in one way or another. The loop is a visual demonstration of your timing, and timing is what it's all about.

Most novices start their practice casting on the lawn, though if you have a pond or swimming pool to play with, so much the better. (It doesn't really make much difference unless you are using sinking line or practicing your roll cast, which works better on real water.) It doesn't take a great deal of room, or much preparation—simply rig up your rod, omitting the leader and fly at first if you wish, and get started. Rigging the rod is simpler if you strip off about 15 feet of line, double the last foot or so of it and walk that through the guides. The doubled line won't slip all the way back through the guides if you should happen to drop it as you feed it through, and somehow, this seems to occur fairly frequently.

Incidentally, there is much to be said for adding a leader and fly as soon as you have overcome your initial clumsiness, for this will keep reminding you of two most important factors: that the presentation of the fly is the important thing, and that what happens behind you is just as important in casting as what happens in front. "Look behind you to see where your back cast must go" is a cardinal rule of fly fishing, and you will probably decorate a lot of trees and bushes with your flies before you learn to observe it automatically. Thus there is no point in learning sloppy habits at the beginning, and a fly on the end of your line will quickly remind you of where your back cast is.

You start the cast with the line lying straight out on the grass (water) before you and the rod pointing forward. You start bringing the rod tip up and the line starts sliding toward you. You accelerate the upward motion and throw the line back over your shoulder. As it begins to straighten out in back you change the direction of the rod and bring it forward smartly, pointing the rod in the direction in which you want the cast to go. Now the line that has been back over your shoulder rolls out of its loop and heads forward, forming another loop going in the other direction. When that loop straightens, the line is stretched out in front of you, and it drops to the water. That's a cast.

That's all there is to it; but books have been written about how it's accomplished. Hitting a golf ball is a pretty simple operation too, but doing it so as to get the results you want has been the subject of countless pages.

In a couple of hours of practice on a lawn you should learn to cast well enough to catch some trout, but your eventual development is almost unlimited. It's true that you can be casting in 20 minutes with a good instructor, and maybe with none, but you may also continue to develop for that many years. (So might a golfer, but it's pretty obvious that some go a lot further than others.) Anyway, if you're in reasonable physical condition I'll guarantee that you can learn to cast adequately and in a short time. By that I mean you can lay the fly on the water 30 or 40 feet away and the trout probably won't catch you at it.

The power is applied to the rod through a rather short arc. If we say your head is at 12 o'clock on a clock's face, most of the force of the cast is between 11 o'clock (in front of your face) and 1 o'clock (behind your head). This doesn't mean the rod may not go through a wider arc—simply that the force is applied in that short segment of it. When you pick up the line to cast, the lift may begin with the rod pointing straight out in front of you, and on the back cast it may be allowed to "drift" back over your shoulder, but most of the power is applied in that short arc.

It's common for beginning casters to drop the rod tip too far behind them, and some of them will actually hit the ground or water with the tip in getting added "swing." This not only doesn't help with the cast, it actually fouls up their timing and causes the back cast to fall. Novices will catch this error themselves if they remember that suggestion to look back as well as forward. It's been stated that the caster should wait until he feels the "tug" of the line straightened out behind him before he starts his forward motion. It's true that he should feel the weight of the line back there as it slides through the "loop"; but if he really waits for a tug he has waited too long, for the rod tip should start forward while the fly and front of the fly line are still going back. The proper feel is almost fluid, and any jerks usually mean something is going wrong.

The "pickup" is simply the business of getting the line into the air and headed backward without letting it fall. It starts slowly but accelerates rapidly, and as the line leaves the water and starts over the shoulder, the wrist or arm movement is often described as a "flick" or a "snap." I have no better word, but I don't want it to sound like a jerk.

Proper timing is generally accomplished with wrist and forearm working together, although it is possible to cast with the wrist alone and the forearm held rigid. In long casts, the upper arm, and the entire body for that matter, can be employed. It doesn't matter where the power comes from as long as the timing is correct. To begin with, I'd try to do it mainly with my wrist, with some assist from the forearm.

For decades it was taught that a good caster used only his wrist and should be able to hold a book between his elbow and ribs. Such a system will work, but is needlessly restrictive. Most anglers using very light rods in delicate fishing do nearly all of their casting with their wrists. Almost all of them use more arm with heavier rods and for long distances. Tack hammers and sledgehammers are different tools.

Two paradoxical errors generally show up with beginning casters. First, they try to practice with such a very short length of line that they get no action out of the rod and the motions are actually more difficult. Then, once they think they have the hang of it, they try to see how much line they can keep in the air and gain little but fatigue from that exercise. To begin with, you want to use a modest length of line; 20 to 30 feet is usually enough for you to tell what you're doing. When you are making the loops form properly and everything feels right, stay with that combination for a while. Then, once you have the feel of proper timing, you'll be surprised how easily it can be applied to more line. With considerable practice, the little differences in timing with various rod, line and distance combinations will become automatic.

I have carefully saved mention of human capabilities until this point. I have never seen a physically normal person who could not learn to cast. However, we weren't all created equal in the matters of reflexes, strength and casting aptitude. Some new casters get the knack almost immediately, but some of the relatively slow learners are the smoothest operators in the end. Not all natural athletes come through fast with the fly rod, and big, powerful men sometimes try to do by main force what should be done with finesse. In my experience, women learn the basic moves at about the same speed as men, but they don't like to practice and are passed by the men in the advanced stages. Many men will stand and practice on a football field or lawn by the hour, but very few women will.

The poetic curl and reach of a properly cast fly line can be one of the most charming aspects of trout fishing, and the knack of doing it right, together with all the refinements for special conditions, is a challenge that goes well with skilled fishing. So let's push a little further with the casting business.

The basic cast is simply picking up a length of line from the water (or from the lawn in practice), throwing it back over the shoulder so that it forms the proper loop and then laying it out again. All other moves are based on that procedure, but the refinements come quickly once the basics are accomplished.

The left hand (for a right-handed caster) becomes more and more important as skill progresses. By pulling on the line between the reel and the first, or stripping, guide, you can accent the power of the rod, and that is called "hauling." Its first use will be in picking up a length of line for a cast. As the rod tip begins to sweep up with the line moving toward it on the water, the left hand briskly pulls a foot or so of line through the guides, adding to the speed of the pickup. Since line speed is what you're dealing with in all casting, this can make things decidedly easier.

All right. The left hand pulls some line through the guides as the line is picked from the water and goes back over the shoulder and into a proper loop. Then when the rod is pushed forward to make the cast, the line that has been held in the left hand is released so that it can be pulled through the guides by the line's momentum. The cast is still the same length as it was before, but the line speed has been increased by the single haul.

When the left hand feeds line through the guides as the cast is made, it is called "shooting," and in most distance casting a great deal of shooting is involved. Let's go on to make more use of the haul and the line shooting that goes with it.

Now you pull a little additional line from the reel and let it hang loosely from the left hand. As before, you pick up the line from the water, hauling a little with the left hand, and make the back cast. Then as the forward, or "fishing," cast takes form and is going forward at top speed, you release your hold on the line held in your left hand, and the weight of the line going forward pulls out not only the short length of line that you hauled in while picking up from the water, but also the extra line that you had pulled from the reel. That is a single haul and a shoot. Now the cast is longer by the length of the extra line that you have shot. As the extra line is shot through the guides it is allowed to run across the fingers of the left hand, and you may want to form a complete circle with your thumb and a finger.

If you have shot considerable line, you probably have more of it out than you can conveniently pick up for another cast, so you must retrieve some of it before beginning the pickup. To do that you strip it in with the left hand. The best way is to pull the line under one or

Laying out the forward loop and shooting a little line. As soon as the cast is completed, this angler will slip a finger of his rod hand over the line and start stripping it with his left hand.

two fingers of the right hand as it grasps the cork grip. Those fingers can serve as a brake to keep the line from slipping back out. Then the left hand, held "below" the right, does the stripping in a series of pulls. This is the accepted form for most retrieving, and the slack line falls to the ground or into the water, to be shot on a later cast.

Already you are performing nearly all of the essential movements of advanced fly casting, even though it may take you a long while to perfect their use. None of the moves are gimmicks, but some of them are skipped by self-taught anglers; they may find they have to add them late in the game, when new practices come hard. For example, the simple method of retrieving line (bringing it between the fingers of the right hand and the grip, with the left hand doing the pulling and using the right hand as a brake or stop when needed) is not absolutely necessary in much trout fishing. I once fished with one of the country's finest trout anglers who had been catching educated trout for 40 years but who had not learned that procedure. When he'd wanted to take up line fast without using his reel, he'd always simply reached up to the stripping guide with his left hand, pulled back several feet of line, hooked it with a finger of his right hand and then reached for the guide again with his left. That can serve when you're just hauling line in, but when you're making a retrieve and want to manipulate a fly, the business of pulling the line through the rod hand is invaluable. I'll say more about retrieves later, but the proper form is best learned at the beginning.

Before leaving the business of line hauling, I may as well also discuss the double haul. This is an advanced procedure which will add a great deal of distance to the cast in most cases and is a frequent topic in fly-casting talk. However, you can fish successfully for a lifetime without doing it, and it should be left until last, for it can be confusing to stick it into the practice too soon.

The double haul is a matter of pulling on the line twice with the left hand, both as the line is picked up and again as it is thrown forward. This is a pretty complicated thing to learn for most fishermen, though others who have no better reflexes or aptitude get the feeling of it quickly, possibly by accident. Here's how it's done:

As you start to pick the line from the water, you haul with your left hand normally, adding speed to the pickup. Then when the line has carried back over your shoulder and the loop has formed on the way back, you feed line through the guides and let the loop pull it back into the back cast. As the rod swings forward, pulling the line toward the fishing cast, the left hand hauls a second time, now adding speed to the fishing cast. Just as the fishing cast begins to "turn over," or straighten its loop, the left hand releases the line and allows it to shoot. Properly executed, this procedure can make for very long casts, but for most of us it's like patting the head and rubbing the stomach at the same time.

Many instructors abhor the thought of mentioning the double haul to beginning casters, but I see no reason for keeping it a secret; you may pick it up very easily. However, if it comes hard or not at all at first, don't worry about it. It is convenient but it is not essential, and you can add it later when other moves have become second nature.

(Some of these things become so automatic through long use that experienced anglers forget how hard it was to learn them in the beginning. Just now, while discussing elementary line hauling, I had to string up a rod and step out into the yard to see how I do it. That was a humbling experience, and I should remember it anytime I expect someone to learn it instantly.)

Although all casting employs the same basic principles, there are special conditions which require modifications. For example, a sidearm cast is very useful for casting under branches or for keeping under the wind. This is done just the same as the conventional cast except that the loop unrolls horizontally rather than vertically. In silhouette, it is the same. A backhand cast also works the same way except that the back cast is made over the other shoulder, across the caster's body. This makes it much more difficult for most fishermen.

No fly caster can ignore the wind, although the expert is much less bothered by it than is the beginner. It's easier to cast with it than against it, but a following wind can be pretty troublesome too. Let's look at some of the modifications necessary to handle winds from various directions.

Casting almost directly into the wind requires a smaller, or tighter, loop, which provides less wind resistance than the normal one. You'll often cast sidearm when casting into the wind because of two advantages: you expose the line to the wind for a shorter time,

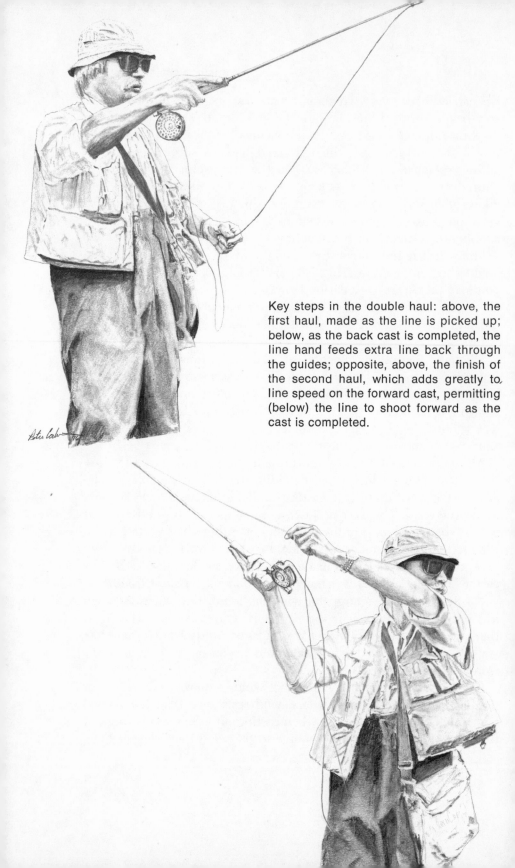

Key steps in the double haul: above, the first haul, made as the line is picked up; below, as the back cast is completed, the line hand feeds extra line back through the guides; opposite, above, the finish of the second haul, which adds greatly to line speed on the forward cast, permitting (below) the line to shoot forward as the cast is completed.

and the line will have a shorter distance to fall to the water when straightened out near the surface with the rod tip low. For a right-hander the worst wind is from the right side and from the front. Not only must the caster overpower the wind, but his line will tend to come close to his ear on the fishing cast (and although all instructors preach keeping the back cast high, nobody always does it, especially in the wind).

To cope with these problems, when the wind comes hard from the right you must make some casting adjustments, and the two most useful ones are almost exact opposites. For short distances you can cast sidearm with the rod almost parallel to the water's surface, the length of the rod keeping the line and hook from getting too familiar. But when the casts get longer the fly will blow into your neck anyway, so you go to the other extreme: You work the line high but with the rod tip tilted to your left, so that the casting is actually done on the left side of your head. Thus, no matter how far off course the fly is blown, it still won't hook you. To cast this way you'll have to keep the casting hand high and it's more work, but at least you can do some fishing.

I am cautious about using confusing names for the various kinds of casts, but the "wind cheaters" are pretty descriptive and work on winds coming from nearly directly ahead or nearly directly behind. If the wind comes from nearly straight ahead, you simply toss your back cast extra high and let the breeze straighten it out up there. Then, coming forward, you drive hard down toward the water; since the wind is coming from that direction, your line is still not likely to slap down too loudly. When the wind comes from almost directly behind you, you make your back cast with a tight loop and rather low; then throw your fishing cast as if you were sending it almost straight up. The wind from the rear will take it forward in a big loop and straighten it out.

The "change-direction" cast is used when, let's say, you've been fishing to the north and want to fish to the east without taking in your line and starting all over. You can, of course, make a series of false casts while you gradually turn your body to the new direction, or you can throw a single back cast with a sort of circular motion as you turn to face the new fishing direction. Then you drive the cast pretty hard. It may not be pretty, but it'll generally get you into action facing east.

The "steeple cast" is executed when obstructions at your back make it impossible to throw a normal back cast. The "steeple" back cast is simply thrown extra high (I'd like to say "straight up," but it won't really go like that) so as to take up less room behind you. Then you cast forward normally.

The "roll cast" has been described endlessly, and often unsuccessfully. It too is used when there's no room for a back cast, and while very few fishermen can make a long roll cast, almost all can make a short one. It's a very useful cast, and not really very complicated. With the line lying extended on or in the water and the rod pointed in the same direction, you simply raise the tip slowly, so that the line starts coming toward you. Then, instead of tossing it over your shoulder, as in normal casting, you continue the rod movement at the same speed until the tip is slightly behind the vertical, with the line hanging down from it and bellying slightly to the rear. Now make a brisk forward movement with the rod tip, and the line will come up off the water and shoot forward in an arc. Most fishermen can roll-cast only 30 feet or so at best, but mainly because they haven't practiced it much. Some steelhead fishermen can get 90 feet with specialized equipment.

In many kinds of trout fishing, especially with dry flies, it is necessary to lay the fly and line on the water very gently. A long and light leader helps in this, but the way the cast is delivered is especially important. When there is no interference from wind, the perfect cast can be straightened out just above the water, and the leader and line then drop together, scarcely disturbing the surface. Perhaps the ideal picture-book presentation would find the fly alighting before the leader and line, but if they come down together there's no complaint. In any event, a delicate presentation makes it necessary to aim the fly at a point slightly above the water, and the leader should roll out so that it is completely extended just before it falls.

If the leader and line never straighten out but fall into the water in a heap, it means either that the cast has been made downward against the water or that too much line has been thrown without enough power and timing to straighten it. The remedy is either to aim the cast a little higher, in the first instance, or to cast a little less line, in the second. In the second case, when the caster is going for distance, it is possible that he has shot too much line—in other words, he fed too much line through the guides on the fishing cast and did not have enough power to "turn the cast over." The same sloppy presentation can occur when he tries to false-cast too much line and the whole thing fails to shape up into loops.

When the leader and fly strike the water too hard with a splat, it can be a result of casting hard without having enough line out to absorb the power, or of throwing the cast downward toward the water. Too short a leader can cause this problem too, as I will discuss in more detail later.

When the fly and/or line strikes the water or ground behind a caster, it is usually a result of exerting power too far back with the rod during the back cast—that is, thrusting the tip so far back that it heads the back cast down instead of up. Trying to carry too much line in the air will also cause it to sag and strike the water. A high wind can blow it down, and poor timing can cause it, too. Except for the time problem, these faults are easily noticed. Very few of us keep our back casts as high as we think we do, and while a truly high back cast may not be necessary, a really low one means trouble. That trouble can strike with a vengeance when a fisherman has been casting sloppily from a boat or from very shallow water and then wades in above his waist. He may have to change his casting style completely, and his problems are accentuated by the fact that he must now hold his elbows out of the water. A fairly low back cast may cause no trouble, but it's almost impossible to get one too high.

Keeping the rod moving in a vertical plane has some effect in holding the back cast up, but I have noticed that a large proportion of the practical casters use a little sideswipe, and it apparently does no harm in the final analysis. If it's more comfortable to tip the rod a little away from your body, go ahead. All of us tend to acquire little sloppy moves that aren't quite classic but feel good to us, and if it's a strain to do it otherwise, it may be that your way is less tiring for you.

False casting (working the line back and forth without allowing it to fall) is essential in getting out the amount of line to be used, and also in drying off dry flies in the air. Experienced casters will make a false cast now and then to make sure their line is working properly, but the common failing of the beginner is to whip the air constantly for reasons he's not quite sure of himself, making a lot of extra work for nothing.

Unless you are waving a floating fly to dry it, there are few instances in trout fishing when more than one false cast is necessary, and in most situations none at all is needed. When casting in tournaments, accuracy throwers often make repeated false casts to be certain the fly is in the correct plane to drop on the target, and in true long-distance casting there are many false casts to make certain that the long line being carried is forming into a proper loop. But in fishing, such operations not only become a lot of work toward the end of the day, but keep a fly in the air when it should be on the water, where a fish can see it. There are no fish in the air!

It's easy enough for me to say that if you're casting correctly it won't tire you out, but until you get the timing right, an all-day session can be hard on you, regardless of your physical equipment; big, powerful people often offset their muscular advantage by fighting the tackle that much more. I repeat, however, that if everything works properly, your feet or seat should get tired before your arm does.

Fatigue is an important factor in causing fly-fishing dropouts, and I wish I could be more definite about its causes. Ability to cast easily comes with practice, and special muscular development is only a minor factor—like a bicycle rider, a caster never forgets how. Oh, he can be a little rusty, but 20 years without touching a rod won't keep him from doing a pretty good job within 5 minutes.

One trouble spot can be the rod hand. I have known athletic men who acquired some impressive blisters after long sessions with powerful rods, even after long experience in fly fishing. To make it more confusing, the blisters are not in exactly the same place with the different victims. A fly-fishing authority who has written a great deal on the subject once told me that it was easy to recognize a fly fisherman's hand. Down on the heel of the palm, he said, there would be a big callus, appearing as a hard lump. I immediately examined my own right hand, found the lump was there and wore it with pride. But that was many years ago, and although I fish just as much as ever, the lump gradually disappeared, never to return in at least 15 years. The explanation is that I can't possibly be casting the way I used to, even though I don't see any difference. I must be holding the rod grip more lightly, causing less friction as it rocks in my hand during a cast. I still use the most common grip, with my thumb on top of the cork handle.

If you use your wrist a great deal, and even if you do most of your casting with your forearm, the rod *does* move in your hand. As it comes up on the back cast, your fingers should open slightly and the grip shouldn't contact your palm too firmly. I *believe* the blisters and calluses are caused by gripping too tightly, and with better timing and increased confidence the hand relaxes more.

There are other aches and pains you can get with a fly rod. Some fishermen get sore elbows and wrists, and casting often aggravates arthritis. But I know a man with a stiff wrist who casts only with his forearm and a fellow with a smashed elbow who casts with his wrist. It takes a little adaptation. Thus though I preach basic methods, I am aware there are many ways of casting a fly.

After learning to cast adequately you will become more conscious of the various types of fly lines. The double-tapered and level lines are not intended for distance casting, but you'll find that you can "carry more line in the air" with them. The forward-tapers are intended more for shooting and don't work well with much more than the "head," or large part, of the line being false-cast. It's a matter of the back part of the line's being too light to help hold the heavy part in the air. It sounds complicated, but it pops out plainly as soon as you start using the various types.

When a fly is actually in the water, the best attitude of the rod is pointed parallel to the surface or slightly upward and not quite in the same direction as the line. For a right-handed fisherman, the rod should generally be pointed to the right of the fly. This will permit the angler to set his hook smoothly, and means that a sudden, hard strike will not be so likely to break the leader, since it would thus encounter some give from the rod tip.

After catching hundreds of smaller fish one can become sloppy about this rod position, but it's a good policy to go on the assumption that every fish will be a big one, even if you're fishing where nothing over a foot long has been sighted for years. It will save some embarrassing incidents. Most of the big trout I've lost have gotten away because of my carelessness or stupidity.

I still wince at recollection of a long, hard day of fishing at a spot where a river flowed into a lake. Fish weren't too frequent, but they were very large, and I'd caught a 6-pounder, a rainbow natives assured me was hardly worth weighing. I was wading rather deep and when I moved a few feet I gave full attention to that, leaving my streamer in the water with my rod carelessly pointed straight at it. Of course, that was the moment when a really heavy fish struck hard, snapping the leader instantly. I wish that were the only instance of such foolishness on my part!

Playing and landing fish is more a matter of presence of mind and knowing what the tackle will stand than any mysterious trick of manipulation. Most of the essentials, especially a sense of the strength of your tackle, can be learned in a few minutes on dry ground. Tie your leader to something solid and then break it or try to break it by bending your rod at about the angle it would assume

A hooked rainbow leaps high in a valley stream. The fisherman is Dan Bailey of trout-fly fame.

if you were playing a fish. In this exercise you'll probably be astonished to discover how much steady pull a light leader will take and how easily it will break with a little jerk. Most break-offs occur when there's a jerk, caused by either the fisherman or the fish, and in many cases it occurs when the leader is already taut. Under such circumstances the fatal jerk is sometimes barely felt, and occasionally not at all. When you check on your leader strength, be sure to use at least two different sizes you're likely to fish with.

Most fish playing is done with the rod grip approximately at a right angle to the fish, regardless of how the tip bends. Here are a few of the rules:

In most cases you set the hook with a quick lift of the rod tip. However, if you jerk it too quickly the tip will bend toward the fish before it pulls on him. In such cases the setting isn't as fast as you thought it would be and when the line does come taut, it does so with an abrupt jerk. The left hand should assist in setting the hook by briskly taking up a little line. The division of labor between the left hand and the rod tip depends upon the individual and the way he's fishing. Too much slack line is a cause of many missed fish, and slack line is especially likely in some forms of dry-fly and nymph fishing.

In streamer fishing there is seldom much slack, and the nature of the lure causes the fish to set the hook himself, much of the time. In most streamer fishing the tackle is not as delicate as with other flies, and hook setting is a fairly automatic process.

Expert anglers usually land fish much more quickly than beginners do. They put on more pressure, because they have a better idea of what the tackle will stand and they know that the longer a fish is on the more things can go wrong. The fact is that most anglers fishing with a leader that tests 4 pounds or less seldom put as much as a pound of stress on it, exclusive of accidental jerks. Tiny hooks, of course, will usually stand less pressure than larger ones, but many a fisherman is astonished at how hard it is to extract a No. 18 once it's firmly embedded in a trout's jaw or tongue. (It is also very difficult to get out of a fisherman's ear.)

On anything but the very lightest tippets, a trout less than a foot long probably won't take line from you. You simply keep the tip high, and although the fish may jump and dart about, it is likely to

Harry (Red) Murray plays a brown trout on the Letort in Pennsylvania. Note that at this point the fish is "on the reel" with no line held in the left hand—important with heavy fish that might lunge suddenly. Thick vegetation is landing hazard.

become tired within a few seconds and come to the surface, where it can be skidded to your net or hand.

You can play most small fish with the extra line you have in your left hand and work them in without using your reel, but when the fish is large the first rule is to "get him on the reel"—that is, get all loose line collected on the spool and play the fish with the reel only. Otherwise, it is impossible to play a catch with even pressure and to avoid jerking. In addition, excessive line handled by hand will often get tangled or looped over something—even the rod butt or reel. And it's easier to step into it than you'd think.

Only very large trout or salmon require much of a drag on the reel, and in most cases all you need is a little smooth and even restraint, the rod bending so that the friction of line through the guides puts on pressure enough. It's seldom necessary to adjust the drag while a fish is on. When you must add pressure briefly, you can run the line through your fingers. Admittedly, big salmon and steelhead require slight shifts in tactics, but most fishermen start with something smaller and are ready for the big ones when the time comes.

A fly rod is "pumped" when a fish is being brought in, just as in most other forms of fishing. The tip is raised without giving line, and when it is as high as practical, it is dipped toward the fish and line is taken up on the reel. Then, with the reel stopped, the tip is raised again, pulling the fish for another few feet, and the reeling and rod lowering take place again.

When a fish jumps against a tight line, the rod tip should be lowered to avoid a hard jerk, which is called "bowing to the fish." Frankly, this procedure is generally used more with very large fish; the smaller trout, leaping in shallow water, is likely to be into the air before you can start your concession to him. A large proportion of fishermen just hang on during leaps, and unless the trout throw the hook, I don't think many are lost in the air. A fly is not as easy to throw as a heavy lure. Spin fishermen or plug casters have more worries about jumps.

Fly reels can be mounted so that the handle works on either the right or the left side, and although I don't think the matter is vital to the world's course, it's a decision to be made, with reasons for either system. If a right-handed fisherman mounts his reel so that it can be cranked with his left hand, he always has his reel fingers close to the handle and he need not change hands with his rod in order to reel. This, the proponents say, makes the whole thing simpler, and in playing a fish you handle the rod with the more responsive, stronger and better-educated fist. There's another side to it, though.

If you have the reel handle on the right side you change hands with the rod at intervals, thus giving your right hand and arm a rest. Also, some of us can wind much faster with the right hand than with the left. (I'm one of those, and nearly twice as fast right-handed.) There are reels specially made for right- or left-hand operation and a few that can be reversed. For 30 years I wound with my left hand

and then switched to the right-hand handle, but I don't feel my life has been drastically changed.

Most fish fights come out something like this: As soon as he's hooked the fish makes whatever runs he's capable of; does his jumping, if any, and then comes to the surface because of the relentless lift of the rod. He'll probably thrash about on top and probably won't start any very long runs, but is capable of a quick trip or two even then. But if he's not landed soon after he comes to the surface he begins to revive, and a big one may be able to swim stubbornly for as long as the fisherman's patience can last, possibly wearing the hook hole larger and eventually getting away. It's best to add pressure when he comes up on top and land him as soon as possible after that.

With heavy fish in swift water there are some complications but also some helpful factors. Since a trout in swift water spends most of his time facing upstream, that's the way he is most likely to head upon being hooked, and also the procedure that will tire him quickest. Of course, he's much harder to hold if he does go down-

Angler detaches landing net from French snap attached to vest. Net hangs between the shoulder blades while angler is casting and can be unfastened with one hand. The fish is a brown trout in a quiet stream where light leaders are necessary.

stream, and you'll probably have to let him take considerable line. But in most cases the fish gives out while headed upstream and is likely to simply ride down with the current as a nearly dead weight. I've followed more nearly exhausted fish than I have fresh ones because the victim is often too large to be pumped up against the current. You must get below him and pull him to shore, or you must hang on and hope he swings to the bank.

A large fish is likely to hold in fairly swift water, transmitting powerful tugs to the rod. In most cases he has his nose down behind a submerged boulder, and with real whoppers, this can become a test of tackle. You can't leave him there indefinitely, and if for some reason you can't get below him to dislodge him, you have to haul him out sideways or upstream.

After losing a carefully played fish I've often concluded that there's no right way to do it, and after some clumsy efforts that turned out right I felt there was no wrong way. A typical bit of advice from a master fisherman is "Pour it on him, but not too much!" Within 20 seconds I have been told by the same man to tighten up a little and ease off a little, and did neither. If we have to be flowery about it, I guess the proper attitude toward a hooked fish is restrained aggression. Force him, but not too much, and beyond that I think I'm wasting your time.

Atlantic salmon and some Pacific salmon are occasionally gaffed, but most trout are landed with a small net or by hand. The netting procedure is about the same regardless of the fish. Submerge the net, pull the fish over it and net the fish headfirst, for his reverse gear is inefficient. Swatting at him or chasing a fish with a net may knock him off and might scare him so badly he'll find new reserves and start the fight all over again. Taking the leader in your hand invites a break-off, because you lose the forgiving flexibility of the rod.

In netting or hand-landing a trout, you usually push the rod handle back behind you or out to one side so that the rod will not be so sharply bent. Since the knot of leader to line may be lumpy, it's best if you can keep all of the leader out past the tip, as the knot might catch if the fish makes a sudden pull.

In water more than knee-deep you can pull a fish against your leg and hold him there to be released or to be grasped in a firmer hold.

Netting a heavy trout in fast water. This fish has been worked to exhaustion and then netted while facing upstream. A fish should be netted headfirst, and a small net will work if the catch is tired.

Smaller fish can be held firmly with thumb back of gill covers. This brown took a Muddler Minnow.

If you're going to kill him, you can grab him by the gills. You can land some trout by putting the hand over them from above, the fingers pressing down the gill covers. In a sort of "soft hand" operation it is also possible to lift a trout loosely with your hand under his belly; when he squirms you simply juggle him instead of clamping down. Sometimes I do it right and sometimes I fumble. Any way

Caster using "conventional" steelhead tackle prepares to beach a 15-pound steelhead. When fish is sufficiently tired it will be skidded to bar. Soft-tipped rod is designed for delicate operation of "bobber"-type bottom lures. Angler is Sam Langlois, West Coast steelhead veteran.

you do it, a trout makes a career of slipperiness, and everybody drops one sometimes.

Though may experts hand-land their fish by using the above methods, I generally use a net, especially when the fish are small and I expect to release them. Fish that are to be released must be handled very gently if they are to survive, and this is easier if they are wrapped in the mesh of the net before you attempt to remove the hook. A good disgorger or pair of forceps also aids hook removal, but if you know you are going to release fish, it is better still to compress the barb of your hooks against the shank in advance with a pair of pliers.

Fish brought to net quickly have a much better chance of survival. Very tired fish should be supported upright and moved gently back and forth to get their gills working before being completely released. In all such operations, remember that most fish are damaged by being squeezed too tightly. Above all, if you intend to release the fish, avoid handling the gills.

"Beaching" generally suggests very large fish, but it works on all sizes if the banks are right. Most of the bigger trout, steelhead and salmon I've caught were beached. The idea is to lead the fish to very shallow water where his own flopping or swimming will get him farther from safety. A sand or gravel bar is perfect, and it's usually possible to find a gently sloping bank. Incidentally, once he is on his side it's surprising how large a fish can be towed by a relatively light leader, possibly to dry ground. If you really want him you can sometimes scoop him with your hands for the last 2 or 3 feet, and it's sometimes possible to kick him out. My jaw dropped the first time I saw a 20-pound steelhead place-kicked up into the grass. But if it's not a very elegant technique, it can come in handy every now and then.

5

UNDERSTANDING TROUT WATER

Any study of trout must start with the premise that they are generally facing upstream. This is a condition that experienced fishermen take for granted, but nonanglers sometimes ask how we know it. It's a simple matter of the way a trout is built; his reverse gear isn't very strong, and if he didn't face upstream most of the time, he'd be washed away.

It follows that "reading water" is considerably simplified by knowing which way the fish are headed, the fact that most food comes from upstream, and a little information about the way fish see. Since a trout's eyes are placed pretty well at the sides of his head, there is only a small area to the front in which he has binocular vision and good depth perception, and biologists tell us that his sharpest vision is to the side. There is a "blind" area to the rear, making it easier to approach the fish from there without being seen. However, even when he's facing upstream he'll frequently move so that he "looks back" while in the process of feeding or working the current. The trout haven't told me, but I have noticed that nonfeeding fish shift position occasionally, and I suspect it's for a look over their shoulders.

A study of trout vision isn't very exciting to someone anxious to hook a fish, but a few of the elements are pretty essential—not only for the purpose of delivering a fly or lure, but in order to avoid scaring your subject out of range while you're walking, wading or boating.

Given a completely calm surface—which isn't common on trout water—a trout has excellent vision of floating objects immediately above him in what is called his "cone of vision." The deeper he lies in the water, the wider his field of acute surface vision, although there's a point at which water clarity will become a factor, muddy water being bad news for the angler with dry flies. Now, a calm surface outside the perimeter of the fish's "vision cone" would serve as a mirror, and in it the fish can see the bottom reflected for a wide area about him, so he "sees some parts of the bottom twice" and can make out some features in the reflection he might not see directly. He could see the other side of a boulder, for instance, by looking at the surface above it. If an insect happens to be floating outside his cone of vision, it might be visible only as a little depression, or "blip," in the surface film.

If he's close enough, he can see the legs of a wading fisherman in great detail. Because of complex light refraction, he sees above-surface things in a distorted way—but the higher the object, the less the distortion. Thus a fisherman's waving rod might frighten fish when the fisherman himself wasn't noticed. Motion is noted when a stationary object isn't.

The ways in which trout feed are good to know, and watching the process in a clear stream is time well spent, especially if there's a good insect hatch. The little fish act much the same as the big ones, and even hatchery trout are worth watching if you can't watch wild ones.

A trout is territorial when not engaged in migration and is likely to use the same feeding station day after day, a place that may be apart from its resting area but could be the same. Fishermen have caught the same fish repeatedly from the same spot. I've seen that happen during one season, and angling literature is filled with in-

Using a dry fly over boulder water. The deepest, swiftest flow is against the opposite bank.

stances of the same big fish appearing on station year after year— the sort of thing that causes some fishermen to prefer the same water for a lifetime.

Generally, a feeding station is near the bottom, although there are times when a fish will be so busy taking flies or shallow nymphs that it will hang near the surface for considerable periods. Given a suitable supply of food coming down the current, the area covered from a feeding station may be quite small. Estimating the area covered in feet and inches is bound to bring cries of outrage from those who disagree, but let's put it into some kind of perspective. I have watched trout lying in 3 feet of water with a hatch of insects coming down over them when the area from which they would take naturals might cover no more than 2 square feet. In other words, the fish would intercept floating flies in a zone no bigger than a foot wide and 2 feet long (up and down stream).

That's the ideal situation, from the trout's viewpoint. If the flies are scarce he will go farther for them, and there are undoubtedly times when trout cruise almost constantly, even in fast water, but if you think in terms of feeding stations you'll do a better job of fishing. There are good trout streams where you may never see a trout until it's on your hook, and there are productive rivers where you'll never see a definite hatch of any particular insect, but trout do about the same things with or without an audience, and by knowing the procedure you're ahead of the game.

Let's describe a typical feeding situation. The current is brisk but not bumpy, the water is clear and there is a good hatch of small flies floating down. The water is 3 feet deep, and there are enough pockets and large stones on the bottom to cause some current diversion and make it easy for a fish to hold without swimming too hard.

The fish selects a fly—possibly sighting it before it gets into the cone of best vision; maybe seeing only the blip on the surface mirror. From his position slightly above the bottom and facing straight upstream, the fish tips upward and swims forward to meet the insect. At the surface the trout opens its mouth and lets the current carry the insect into it, the water going out through the gills and the insect being diverted down the throat. There is likely to be a bubble or two from the gills as some air goes in with the insect. The trout, having been carried a little back of its feeding station, now swims forward and down to wait for another target. Let's call that a classic rise and return, the fish facing upstream through the entire operation and expending a minimum of effort.

When the insects are scarce and the fish must cover a much larger area in its rises there may be brief disputes over feeding territory—quickly resolved by a darting contact, with the smaller fish moving away. It appears to me that a large trout frequently usurps a smaller fish's territory if the feeding is better there for some reason. Of course wind, water level or the nature of the food supply can cause abandonment of an area. When flies flutter along the surface there may be spirited chases, and when the flies are airborne there are occasional jumps for them.

A very slow or nonexistent current will change the feeding program completely. If the food doesn't come to the fish the fish must go to the food, and when trout are feeding on surface or near-surface objects they will travel considerable distances. A fish may cause a dimple on the surface and be 10 feet away by the time you are ready to cast to him. There's a saying that the one place he *isn't* is where he last broke the surface, but even if you can't see the fish itself you can sometimes establish a pattern of its route. A Michigan angler I knew became especially deadly on an evening rise on a lake. He would study a series of disturbances made by a particular fish, note the length of time and space between rises and estimate exactly where the fish would be ready to rise again. We all do that to some extent, but by fishing the same area continually this fellow had it down to a science.

The touring risers are found on sloughs, lakes and even small backwaters on swift rivers, and they can be very difficult to catch because a placid surface makes leaders or lines highly visible. It can be some of the most delicate fishing in the world.

Such elementary observations of trout behavior are helpful in understanding trout water, for they can provide some insight into general stream features, even though runs, pools, ripples and rapids can mean different things in different kinds of water.

For example, what might be considered a "pool" in very swift rivers would still be moving much faster than a "pool" in a slow stream. When I first read about trout pools, I visualized them as nearly motionless ponds, with moving water upstream and downstream. Thus during some of my first trout trips I looked for deep, blue areas with no noticeable current and assumed that trout would stay there rather than in swift water. As I learned, there are fish in such places, but they are generally very difficult to catch. Swift water looks tougher but it's generally the easiest place to fool a trout if he's present.

To begin the tactics of reading water, you usually divide a pool into its head, or upstream part; the waist, or middle part, and the tail, or lower part, whether the pool is swift or slow. Some trout streams have such a constant speed, depth and width that there are no distinct pools, but many good ones are divided into pools with well-known names, often colorful and some with long-forgotten origins. Pools may be named for an owner or for someone who has been a particularly successful fisherman there, or frequently for some visible feature. Thus come names such as the McLeod Pool, the Boulder Pool and the Bridge Pool. The Earthquake Pool may be harder to nail down after a few generations of fishermen have called it that.

Let us suppose that there is swift current at the head of a pool. It results from a steep pitch, the head being shallower than the pool below it. This swift water probably runs over well-polished rocks, regardless of the kind of bottom found in the rest of the pool, and the lower end of the "headwater" is consistently a location of feeding fish. Competition is one factor; since it's natural for the fish to try to get as near as possible to the food supply, many of them end

Casting into a deep pocket out of the main current, the fisherman puts a dry fly into the shade of streamside willows. This is a small stream at low water, when shade and oxygen are at a premium.

up just where the fast water comes in. Moreover, rocky riffles are most productive of some types of nymphs and the resultant flies, for such areas are not subject to such rapid silting and washing as are muddy or sandy areas, and thus are the most stable parts of a stream.

A typical rocky stream will have the swift water coming in on a sort of stone ramp that slopes down into the main pool. It's been built up by floodwaters, and generally there is an eddy on one or both sides where the water is deeper than in the swift current. Although there may be trout anywhere in such a situation, the most logical place for a good fish is in the edge of the eddy, just out of the current's main thrust. From there the fish can readily go into faster water to feed and then drop back to a holding spot where he won't have to work so hard.

The area in which this very swift water begins to spread out over the pool's bottom, provides another top location for trout, for if the bottom is suitably irregular, they can find nearly motionless water there, even though there's foam, fury and spray above them. A fisherman is well into the game if he remembers that his purpose is to serve up his fly or lure in such a way that it appears to be coming down from above the pool.

Turbulent water is easier to fish than it appears, for it is far more tolerant of error than glassy sweeps of slow current. An artificial nymph coming through broken water behaves much like a live one that has been dislodged from its upstream location, and a dry fly need not be so nearly perfect in its float. (After all, the natural fly can be battered by current too, and many a "dry" has caught fish in such places after being drowned by choppy waves.) Turbulent water also greatly reduces the fish's visual acuity, so that it is more likely to take a fly that wouldn't work in calm pools, less conscious of leaders and capable of seeing the fisherman only when the light is just right. Then too, under some conditions—especially in warm weather—the oxygen content is much greater in riffles, and fish tend to concentrate there for that reason as well. Hence choppy water can make educated trout appear simple, and I have soothed my wounds repeatedly by leaving glassy stretches and seeking easier flows.

One summer on the Firehole in Yellowstone National Park, for

In the high country many trout live in white water, where they can rest only in small pockets and beneath boulders.

example, I was completely frustrated by little pods of rainbows that were cruising slowly in the glassy stretches and taking an underwater *something* I couldn't see. After throwing to them and being ignored for a while I'd hurry to a swift riffle, catch a fish or two for the sake of my morale and then go back to work on the tough ones. I never did get a strike in the calm water. I've done the same cowardly stunt elsewhere.

The tail of the pool generally shelves up, tending to be shallower than the head, and then breaks into faster water as it heads for the next pool. The pool's tail may be quite shallow, and fish there are easily frightened, so some of the best fishing in such water occurs in the evening. In some larger rivers spawning beds are likely to be concentrated near pool tails, because they can provide a good combination of suitable gravel and current.

Fishermen working upstream often stomp carelessly through the pool tails to get at the heavier water. This is a mistake, for though it takes pretty careful stalking, many good trout can be taken in a few inches of depth there. Furthermore, careless treatment of the pool's tail in a small stream can start a chain reaction as fish from the tail hurry upstream and scare others that wouldn't otherwise know a fisherman was present. Remember that even tiny trout you aren't interested in catching can spook fish that you want. Big trout aren't likely to be in the very shallow tails unless they're actively feeding, but little ones will lie in a couple of inches of water.

Most stream trout are caught in water less than 3 feet deep, and many are taken in less than a foot. Those fish taken from water over 6 feet deep are generally caught on deep-going streamers or lures. There are exceptions, but most dry-fly takers do so from shallow water in which they can see the floating flies from lies very near the bottom. Even if they could follow the progress of floating insects from considerable depth, it would be a matter of simple logistics for large fish—too long a trip for too small a package. Most fishermen operate over pretty shallow water even when using nymphs or wet flies, but it takes special equipment and tactics to really probe the depths. We'll discuss deep bottom bumping later. It has its place, but getting a fly down deep isn't quite as simple as it looks.

Obstructions in moving water, whether boulders, old logs or bridge abutments, attract trout, but sometimes for reasons that aren't readily apparent. It's more than just a case of a fish hiding behind a rock. Look at some of the possibilities:

If a big boulder sticks far out of the water, the current will divide, swing around it and close in below it, slowed so much that it may drop what it's carrying and cause a shallow spot where the water is almost stationary. On the other hand, if current pours over a rock or log in just the right way it tends to gouge a deep hole just downstream from it—a characteristic that is exploited by those who improve trout water by construction projects. The vagaries of current in relation to obstructions are such that experienced fishermen are

Midstream boulders like this should be worked carefully. The angler, Mary Shepard, writer and tackle historian, has covered the near side and now lays her dry fly where the current divides on the far side.

very careful with them and make numerous casts before moving elsewhere.

Wherever he is, the fish wants protection from the current and predators, plus access to food. There is a cushion of slowed water above a large obstruction, and that's one good spot for a cast. Below a large boulder and just to either side there is a break between the hard current and the slow and confused turbulence below the rock, and regardless of where the fish is lying, that's the area he is likely to be watching for dinner. You can read some of the characteristics of a large obstruction, and others you can guess at, but remember to work it over well, no matter what you're casting.

Undercut banks shelter many good trout and are sometimes

harder to fish than they appear at first. A fly that sinks can be worked back under with a natural current, but when you're using a dry fly it's quite possible to throw it too close to the bank, where a fish can't see it if he's well back under. Fish beneath such banks probably aren't looking for dry flies, but many feeding stations are just outside the sheltered area.

"Sweepers" are grass or branches that hang into the water from above. Not only do they provide shade and hiding, but terrestrial insects tumble from them, especially in high winds. If the water is deep enough to hold a fish, almost any sweeper is worth your attention.

On bright days trout tend to seek shade, but the love for shade is quickly overcome where there are desired insects that hatch in sun-

Cutthroat trout came from tight against willows on small mountain stream. The cast was made from well back of where the fisherman is now standing.

light. Visible hatch or not, dusk is a time for trout to move, especially into shallows they would not risk in broad daylight. Large trout, especially brown trout, are noted as nighttime feeders.

In this day very few fishermen ever approach a stream without having some confidence that it contains trout, for the water's reputation is probably what brought them to it in the first place. However, selecting the better sections still requires some thought.

Good trout water is characterized by variety, and a watercourse with numerous meanders and a wide range of depths is a better choice than a stretch which impresses with its sameness. It is the bends, bars, shoals and pockets that give the fish a choice, and trout use different kinds of water at different times. Many streams have been straightened as a part of land management with several bad results. It is rare that nature produces a straight channel. When a river becomes a ditch, the most obvious trout problem is the lack of hiding places. In most cases the bottom turns out fairly even, and the banks become too smooth to acquire any pockets, undercuts and eddies, so that the trout must constantly swim for his life with hardly any dead water for resting. Incidentally, if it's a fairly small stream, the fish will also be easily scared, for they can see you approach from almost any direction.

Straightening a stream bed invariably destroys immature insects and insect eggs, thus breaking a pattern of food production. It may take years for the insect hatches to return, if they ever do—and a new stream frequently doesn't have the characteristics for good insect growth.

A straight channel carries floodwaters away too quickly, sometimes washing away insect life with its force, and then when the rain or snow water is followed by drought the channel becomes too slow, shallow and warm. Once you have your waders on and your rod in your hand it may be too late to keep somebody from channelizing your chosen creek, but you can at least avoid the sections with the obvious faults mentioned. I can summarize by saying the crooked places are best.

This large-scale judgment of water becomes especially important when you find yourself in fairly primitive areas without other fishermen as guides. Many an inexperienced angler has spent hours over sterile water when the reason should have been obvious. For example, a healthy trout stream requires sunlight as well as shade, for the sun is essential in much insect growth. There are some very pretty forest creeks where the sun hardly touches water, and the fishing won't be good. And although trout can live in very swift water, there are sections where the current is too overpowering, especially if the bottom is pretty smooth. Remember, too, that some tiny brooks can freeze solid in winter and dry up completely in summer. Unless trout can move up or down to satisfactory water in such emergencies, they won't be there even when the water does look right.

Despite their varied habits in very different waters, trout still have some pretty basic characteristics. Hence a good trout fisherman on one kind of water should develop quickly into a good trout fisherman on other kinds, even though small-stream anglers will often back down from big rivers and big-river anglers may refuse to attempt small and glassy creeks.

There's more polarization in trout fishing than you'd think, and so many possible approaches that you may be surprised by a veteran's complete unfamiliarity with some phases. A few years ago I ran into one of the country's best-known steelhead fishermen working a small creek that required considerable delicacy for persnickety brown trout.

"This is fun," the steelheader said, "and I think I'm going to be able to learn how if I stick with it. I never fished for trout before."

Modesty aside, he recognized that he was into a new game. Note that he didn't even list steelhead as "trout." Anyway, he understood the principles and was a good meadow-stream angler on his second trip.

It usually proves harder to get a small-stream fisherman into big rivers. This is too bad, for though the big river admittedly requires long casts and energetic wading for some streamer operations, when the angler is fishing the dry fly or nymph on light gear it is mentally broken down into a series of small creeks, and the rules are about the same. Many larger rivers run as a unit only part of the time and frequently divide up into several channels, or "splits." Each little channel, in effect, is a small stream with the good or bad characteristics of other small streams, and in a place where the river shallows up and spreads wide there may be half a dozen little runs that can be fished like brooks. Some fine guides have specialized in such fishing, and Ray Hurley, a much-quoted western authority, is one who will take a brook fisherman into a boat, run him through white water and then point out trouty trickles only a few feet from roaring cascades. When the client steps from the boat, he can use the same gear he employs on the creek "back home."

Generally speaking, the dry-fly or nymph fishing in these big rivers isn't as technical as it is in more placid waters. Hatches are generally less predictable, and many of the flies are big. Such trout are opportunists and more inclined to take "attraction" flies which resemble nothing that ever lived, though there are still times when fishing must be fairly delicate.

In big, swift rivers there are times when the fish are almost invariably caught very near the banks, especially if dry flies are used, and fishing from boats works well then. Occasionally, it is a matter of the main current's being too fast.

Red Murray of Virginia fishes a big nymph at the head of a pool on a large western river. He expects action just where the fast water meets slower and deeper current.

The salmon-fly (stone fly) hatch on the upper Yellowstone River in Yellowstone National Park can be an example of that, as I learned when John Bailey and Ben Williams of Livingston, Montana, took me up there one summer. Although the hatch had petered out on the lower parts of the river, it was still going strong in the park; there the river was little more than a series of cascades, and big stone flies were riding the haystacks like canoes out of control. Since the river is in a deep canyon there, we went down with hiking boots and no waders, for where we fished there was no opportunity for wading. We made short casts along the shore, where there were very small eddies and foot-wide patches of quiet water, and cut-throat trout took our giant flies with plops that could be heard over the torrent's roar. I don't recall hooking any fish more than 10 feet from the bank.

You can't cover all of a big river anyway, so you'll do better to think of it piecemeal. Even if your background is exclusively small-stream, a stretch of big water can begin to feel like home when you remember that a fish is in only one place at a time and a boulder in a New Hampshire brook is much the same as a boulder in California's Klamath.

True miniature brooks require a little special attention, for some-times the problem is hitting the water with the fly, let alone putting it on a fish's nose. We tend to think of the eastern brook trout when we consider a check we can step across, although all of the trouts are frequently found there—it's just that the brookie adapts well to close quarters. If a creek is no more than 5 feet wide it's likely a hungry fish can see a fly no matter where it strikes the water. Gen-erally he'll come for it if he wants it, but I have seen times when the fish would move no more than 8 inches from a sweeper, log or bank to take the best presentation I could muster. I cannot explain that.

Reading a very small creek is influenced by the position you're going to fish from. I was fishing for brookies on a very brushy creek in northern Maine one summer, and decided that for once I was going to make every cast count. The fish were small but plentiful, and I was using a little hair-winged Royal Coachman dry fly that the brookies felt was the answer to everything. When I deliberately set up every cast (generally it was only one cast to a pool) so that I would not hang in the bushes, so that my shadow would not fall

Fishing a narrow but deep creek in high country, Ben Williams casts to water he can't even see part of the time. The fish are brook trout.

across the pool and so that my feet would not stir the water, I had a strike on almost every attempt. I ended up crouching on dry ground most of the time and making only fifty casts an hour—but my success ratio was phenomenal.

Much small-creek fishing is really not casting but "dapping," for you simply lower the fly to the water in some brushy stretches, and in such cases a long rod is a help. Since an insect that spills from overhanging grass or brush is apt to fall right in the middle of so small a creek, the fish are always on the lookout for terrestrials. If the grasshoppers are thick where you walk, you have a pretty good indication.

Some very small brooks run through meadows, often through high grass, and the meadow stream is less likely to be divided into distinct pools than a creek with a faster descent. I think distinct pools with shallows between are easier to fish, because you have less chain reaction once you have scared a fish out of its scales. Two of us were beginning operations on a little stream only 2 feet wide but quite deep when I got a jolting demonstration of just how far a spooked fish can carry the alarm. My friend sneaked up on the rivulet a good

50 yards from me, and I was rigging my rod a few feet from the water when he began casting. He hooked a small brookie, and I saw dark streaks passing me at high speed, some of them larger than anything I'd dreamed would live in little more than a wet furrow bordered by grass. By the time those fish had gotten to me, they were stirring the whole creek in their flight. Needless to say, we didn't catch anything very big in that sector.

Since they are highly vulnerable to land-based predators, the occupants of tiny trickles are easily frightened by anything that happens on shore, and some terrain quivers enough with a heavy footstep to stop the fishing momentarily. Livestock in the area is a help, for the trout become used to the vibrations. For that matter, although domestic animals sometimes muddy streams, destroy cover and cave in fragile banks, they make it easier to stalk spooky fish. Distorted by refraction, a fisherman on the bank may look much like a grazing Hereford to a feeding trout, and his footsteps may sound about the same.

Small-creek fishing often involves beaver ponds, impoundments that help some fishing greatly and ruin it elsewhere. Flat statements about them show bad judgment, so let's take a quick look at some of their effects:

Where beaver ponds are recently built and deep they can protect trout from hard freezes, and they can provide cool depths for days that might otherwise raise temperatures past the survival limit. On the other hand, old beaver ponds tend to silt in and become very shallow, restraining a creek's flow until the pond easily becomes hotter than normal or freezes solid (depending on the season) if there's little flow. You can catch some fine trout from the good ponds under proper conditions, using about the same tactics you'd employ on the swifter creek except that you may need to give your flies action that would be supplied elsewhere by the current.

I've had some fine dry-fly fishing by standing on or behind a dam and casting across a small pond to where the creek came in at the upper end. On one occasion it was an old pond, nearly filled with silt, and there were some pretty respectable brookies rising to very small insects in no more than 4 inches of water. By casting from behind the dam, being careful to work from the pond upward, I caught a dozen fish on about that many casts. Brookies aren't noted

A stealthy approach works well at an old beaver dam that holds a deep pool above it. Casting from this angle, the angler is very difficult for the fish to see.

for being selective, and small-creek specimens are generally ready takers. I caught those fish on any small fly I threw.

One of the major points in judging water is its "color," and determining whether or not a given stream is too discolored for a given kind of fishing. It's pretty easy to see that nearly opaque water isn't fishable, but between that and the ancient cliché of "gin-clear," there is food for much argument. Worst of all, a color that would be decidedly "off" for one river might be completely normal and fishable for another, the fish evidently adapting to murkiness in a place where it's a rule rather than an exception. For example, the famous Kispiox, home of giant steelhead in British Columbia, runs a little on the cloudy side even when fly fishing is good. A fisherman might turn away from an eastern brook that looked that way, and the same would go for some high creeks of the Rockies.

Remember that small creeks change much more quickly than big rivers. A hard rain can make a brook too muddy for fishing within a few minutes, whereas it may take a long time for the downpour to have much effect on the river a creek empties into. Don't forget that by the time the river is too muddy, it's possible that the head of the little creek is already clearing. That sounds pretty obvious, but I've known fishermen to travel a long way, look at a river, see that it was chocolate-colored and then abandon the expedition without thinking about tributary streams.

I've fished a great deal and I still get fooled regularly by water conditions, especially the more subtle ones. On the Yellowstone River east of Livingston, Montana, there are some pleasant side channels, nearly always good for dry flies in summer if the river is right. Some of this good water is several miles below the mouth of the Shields River, which often runs muddy when the Yellowstone is clear, and is noted for general cloudiness.

On one summer evening two of us fished everything in the box down below the Shields and raised only a pair of undersized fish. I began to notice that the water was slightly off color, but there have been many times when I've done pretty well on the Yellowstone when it was muddier than that, so I decided it was just a bad day. That night we learned that for other anglers fishing on the big river had been excellent, and it wasn't until I carried my woes to guide Chester Marion that I hit the right explanation. He'd been floating the river regularly and said that the dirty water from the Shields had ruined *that side* of the river for miles downstream. It simply stayed on that bank and didn't mix quickly with the clear river water; even though it caused only a little "color" as far downstream as we were, the fish had apparently abandoned it for the other side of the current. This is a good thing to remember if, like me, you've been thinking in terms of instant mixing. Incidentally, any place where clear water visibly meets cloudy water is likely to be a good fishing spot.

Of course, there are scientific measurements of water clarity, but they are seldom practical for a trout fisherman on streams, especially since it would require long experience before he could decide how much clarity was normal for a given area, but I can state some generalities. If you can stand waist deep in a stream and see your feet plainly, it should be clear enough for any kind of fly or lure. If you can't see your feet plainly in knee-deep water, it's pretty muddy. When deep pools appear blue, the water is pretty clear. If the water appears truly brown or creamy, it's probably too dirty for any kind of artificial lure.

Bait can be used in water far too muddy for successful fly fishing, largely because odor plays a role here. Hardware will catch fish where flies won't work, and streamers are used when dries would fail. The dry fly is considered a clear-water attraction. Off color generally comes with high water and is a typical early-spring condition, so we often say dry flies are at their best on low water. Some nymphs and wet flies will beat dries in off-color water, but they aren't necessarily discontinued when it clears. Now, this is in part a simple matter of visibility, and the fish won't strike what he can't see, but off-color water indicates he won't even be looking for food afloat.

Perhaps a bit of classification would be useful here. Though the terms require a bit of caution, there is a basic distinction between streams that are fed mainly by surface water and those which are fed from underground sources—springs or subterranean rivers. The former, depending on melting snow or rainfall, can have very high water and very low water. They can become muddy quickly if

Water entering stream from spring causes turbulent area ideal for feeding trout.

there's a heavy rain, or hot sun on mountain snows. This means that they change rapidly in appearance and that their courses alter rapidly. (Most river valleys show traces of old beds, long since abandoned by the rivers, and there are sometimes annual changes; these facts have caused endless wrangling over property lines.)

In contrast, the constant-flow trout stream is fed principally by water that has been filtered through earth, stone and vegetation, and its clarity, level and temperature are much more constant than those of the river served by surface water. Of course the levels of all streams change a bit, but the constant-flow stream lacks the erratic ups and downs of a watercourse that depends on surface runoff and is usually clear except in an unusual case, such as an overall flood which sweeps an entire valley or basin.

Another useful distinction concerns acidity, for although a lot of water falls between the two classifications, trout streams are broadly grouped as "freestone" and "limestone." The freestone stream, dependent upon surface water, flows over rocks of volcanic origin and tends toward acidity. It is not nearly as fertile as the limestone stream, which is alkaline and supports a much greater quantity of resident plant and animal matter. Most of the world's most concentrated trout populations are found in limestone waters. The "chalk streams" of England run through a form of limestone. The "spring creeks" of the West are generally limestone.

Insect hatches tend to be heavier and more predictable on the limestone streams, because of their more consistent temperature and volume, but their slow current and extreme clarity may also make fish especially difficult to catch there. Since constant-flow trout streams of any kind aren't very plentiful they are likely to be heavily fished, and since they are not likely to be of much length, they are usually found on private land which is subject to control by owners or lessees.

6

TROUT-FISHING TACTICS

If I were to devise a course of instruction for someone preparing to devote his entire life to fishing for trout with no other occupation, I'd insist that he spend a few weeks doing nothing but wading trout streams. He wouldn't be allowed to fish and wouldn't even have a rod with him. The object of this exercise would be to teach him how to move both up and down stream and approach all good water in such a way that he did not frighten a fish. Anytime he saw a frightened trout darting away he'd get a demerit.

My scholar would assess every spot from which he would cast if he had a rod, and figure how to get the most possible casts from each of them without frightening any fish. Then I'd have him do the same thing while keeping his feet dry, figuring out exactly how he'd cast if he had to do it all from the bank.

All of this sounds like more trouble than any real person is going to take, but I bet it would be worth it. I have an adage that you should fish with your feet as much as with your hands, and in some parts of the world, as on some fine English rivers and in some sections of the Continent, nearly all of the casting is done from shore.

Admittedly, most trout rivers in America are too brushy for that kind of operation, but where it's possible to fish from land, it has decided advantages. I cannot forget the English angler who told me he had been to the Rocky Mountains, "where the Americans wade right up the middle of the rivers—right up the middle of the bloody rivers!" He was appalled at such sacrilege, and although it's certainly advisable to fish that way occasionally, we get into the habit of doing it when it's unnecessary.

Some years ago I was preparing to begin fishing on a placid spring creek that produced good hatches daily when I met a pair of visiting anglers, suiting up by their station wagon. I foolishly volunteered some information about the expected hatch of flies while they gave each other knowing smiles, as if they were listening to a noisy preschooler, and then they walked into the water. ("Walked" may not even be the word, for they sounded like a herd of steers.) They then waded rapidly the half-mile length of the fishing water, side by side, making casts to either shore and keeping their feet moving. That took roughly an hour, after which they removed their waders and left. One claimed to have had a strike, but they caught no fish. A few minutes later the trout began feeding again and it was a fine fishing day. I guess that's what you can call "walking right up the middle of the bloody river!"

I would like to forget a time in Newfoundland when my perceptive guide led me to a pool that consistently held salmon and painstakingly explained the situation. The pool looked too shallow to me.

"The salmon are in a little pocket," he said, "right out there."

I waded in the direction in which he pointed, lengthening my line as I went, and about 30 feet from shore I asked if I could reach the pocket from that point. He may have had to struggle with his temper a little, because he was slow in answering.

"You're standing in it," he said.

The pocket had been a depression of no more than 4 or 5 inches, hardly noted as I sloshed into it—a perfect example of wading carelessness.

On any hard-fished stream of modest size it is easy to tell how your predecessors have waded or walked by observing their tracks.

Working a fallen tree, the fisherman knows that trout are likely to find resting water where protected by the branches. The obstruction also creates a variety of currents which require careful attention and provides shade on hot days.

Generally they have done their casting from obviously logical points, and sometimes you can learn a great deal from their trails. I was very proud of myself one year when Dan Bailey, a really fine fisherman, directed me to a seldom-fished stream in a brushy valley spattered with beaver ponds; as far as I could learn, he had been the only other angler to fish it that year. When I would study a pool and choose a spot to cast from, whether on the marshy bank or in the shallow tail, I'd often find tracks (Dan's wader size) right there, a sure indication that we were thinking alike about pool approach. Of course, if this had been a hard-fished creek with another fisherman only an hour or so ahead of me, these same "logical" spots would have been places to avoid, and some very good fishermen spend considerable time figuring unusual approaches where the pressure is heavy.

For example, it's quite likely that fish holding where everybody walks into the water may never see a fly or lure until they have been pushed somewhere else by a wader. One fish catcher says he makes a practice of working into position to cover such spots first and catches a lot of fish there. It's only natural to walk into the water with your eyes on areas a comfortable cast away, ignoring targets within a few feet.

I've heard talk of "casters" as distinct from "fishermen," meaning that some folks are so obsessed with throwing a line that they forget what they came for, and keep casting their long line right on past the trout. Contrariwise, one of the best trout fishermen I know continually brags about his poor casting ability.

"I can't throw it very far," he keeps saying, "so I make it a rule to get in just the right place before I make a cast."

I privately believe this gentleman gets special pleasure out of catching fish with "poor" casting, for I have noted that when a little distance is *really* needed, he can produce it, but his principles are well taken. The ideal distance for your best fly casting is that at which your rod works well without extra effort. Let's say that with a light trout outfit it's around 30 or 40 feet, and you're generally in fine shape when you can get about that distance from your fish. Your casts will be accurate, you are unlikely to slap the water, you should have no trouble hooking strikes and you're far enough away to keep the fish from reading the trademark on your reel.

Very short casts are awkward for most of us, since the whole principle of fly casting involves having enough line out to bend the rod and make it work. Thus when you're trying to flip a fly only 15 feet you have a special problem and are likely to do something sloppy; it's very hard to cast nothing but a leader. On some very small creeks where nearly all of the casts are short, you may well prefer to use special tackle. The ideal combination is an "overloaded" rod—that is, a rod rigged with line that would ordinarily be too heavy for it. Under these circumstances the rod will work with even very little line through the guides, and keeping the leader as short as possible will also help. A sideswiping cast is often convenient for short distances, because it's good to keep the rod tip out of the sky, and although very short rods have many disadvantages, they can also be a help in a sort of miniature fishing situation.

Now let's think about the upstream–downstream business. The traditional idea is that you fish wet flies and streamers downstream

A classic "spring creek"—the western version of "limestone stream" or "chalk stream." Such waters are alkaline and highly productive of both vegetation and trout. Their uniform flow is conducive to predictable hatches of a variety of insects.

from where you're standing, and fish dry flies and dead-floating nymphs upstream. That means most dry-fly and nymph fishermen plan to wade and walk upstream. They do so because it enables them to approach the trout from the rear and because when the fly is cast upstream, it can float back in a natural dead drift. On the other hand, the streamer and wet fly are often most effective when swung across the current as if they were exerting swimming power of their own, and that's easier done when you're working them downstream.

If you are casting upstream over a good spot or to a known fish, the ideal situation is to lay the fly at an angle to the current. In other words, if the fly is cast from behind to one side of the fish, the leader will not fall over him as the fly arrives, nor will it float over him as the fly drifts downstream. In theory, the fish sees the fly ahead of him and no other equipment is noticed. Before you make another cast over the area, you wait to pick up your fly until it has floated well below the fish so that the pickup won't scare him.

If you cast from directly below the fish your leader will fall over him as the fly alights above him. Sometimes fish are not leader-shy and sometimes the water is turbulent enough for the leader not to make much difference, but you must remember that the slap of a leader coming down awkwardly or the surface rip of it coming up sloppily is more easily forgotten by the fisherman than by the fish. He may have departed for other parts with your first inept cast, and no matter how delicately you proceed after that you may well be fishing over barren water.

Now let's look at some other methods of presenting a dead-drifting fly. If you approach from directly above the trout, the chances are that you'll need to stay a bit farther away from him, as he sees better to the front and has his attention there as he awaits food. The best way to feed a fly straight down the current is to throw it with a slack line that straightens gradually as the fly goes down. You can accomplish that either by waggling the rod as the forward cast is made, or by simply throwing the fly with a weak forward cast that will leave slack, stopping the rod high and then lowering it as the fly and line drift down. In other words, deliberate sloppiness.

This straight-down drift can present the fly almost perfectly. But though the fly arrives ahead of the leader and the leader doesn't fall

Trout has just been hooked in shady area against the far bank. This stream has an abundant crop of watercress and heavy submerged vegetation. It flows through pastureland and is fringed by brush and timber.

near the fish, there are still complications. If there is no strike, the line and leader will eventually drift on over the fish and then must be picked up directly over him. Under some circumstances you get one beautiful chance at him and then you can forget it. There's also a second disadvantage. The best situation for hooking a fish involves pulling the fly into the side of his jaw, and when he takes it straight ahead it's easy to pull it out of his mouth. This is an uncertain area, since the fish may take the fly in a number of ways, but it's enough to say that occasionally you'll miss strikes from directly above.

Most of the exponents of downstream, dead-drift fishing also believe in presenting to the fish at an angle. The cast is made from above and to one side, the fly drifts down over the fish on a little slack and if there is no strike it is then picked up from below his lie so as not to disturb him. Most good fishermen cast both upstream and downstream, regardless of the direction in which they are wading.

A perfect drift, or "float," would be easy if all of the water moved at the same speed. It doesn't, and the big problem is to assess the currents between the caster and the fish and guess what they will do to the fly. Laying a line across fast water but into slow current means that the fast current will whip the line downward and yank the fly into a spectacular drag. This is one of the most valid reasons for careful wading and positioning, and it's the reason why some of the best dry-fly and nymph floats are managed by anglers casting nearly straight upstream or downstream—however awkward for the fishing.

Now, perhaps I've sounded as if the classic "dead drift" were the end-all, be-all of fly fishing. It isn't, though being able to accomplish it is very important. However, there are times, especially on still or nearly still water, when it is desirable to twitch a dry fly or even make it skitter across the surface, and it also helps on some days on fast water. On other days, moving the dry fly won't catch fish for me; and the same things are true of sunken nymphs. Some natural nymphs are good swimmers and others simply squirm a little as they approach the surface to get rid of their shucks, so that manipulation with your rod tip and/or line is often necessary. But sometimes, of course, the deader the drift the better the catch.

In describing these fishing tactics I have possibly made it sound as if you were usually casting to a particular fish you knew about or could see. Most trout aren't seen or known about before they strike, but anytime you are fishing likely water you must assume that you are casting to a fish, and you should guess about where he would be. By thinking this way you'll do a better job, as well as covering water near to you before you make long casts that might scatter nearby fish. The splash of a line and leader is easy for us, if not for the fish, to forget, and many times I have caught myself carefully fishing a spot I'd previously slapped the line over in casting to some other area. Keeping your mind on what you're doing and remembering

Terrestrial imitations are a good choice in this valley stream of the Rockies. On windy days a variety of land insects are blown into the water. Angler tries to keep well back from the target.

what you've done will catch more fish, and thus you'd better suspend your casting while bird-watching or checking weather.

Having said this, I must admit that some of the most educated trout are strangely tolerant of sloppy casting. Take a creek that is hard-fished daily but has a great many fish and you'll find that a sloppy cast may not especially disturb them, probably because they must live in a rain of sloppy casts. That doesn't mean they'll take a poorly delivered fly—simply that they aren't particularly frightened by one. Such fish may pass up a dozen messy presentations and then take a good one. (After all, if they didn't feed while fishermen were working over them, they'd starve.) It is quite possible to catch a feeding fish to which you have shown the same fly a hundred times, and there are famous streams where the average angler moves only a few yards in a day's fishing. In contrast, if it were a secluded river the fish might be more gullible on the first cast, but wouldn't stay around for the second once he saw the line picked up.

Don't confuse this business with "creating a hatch." The "creation" system involves simply throwing a certain fly so frequently in the same place that a fish decides a hatch of that particular pattern is developing and "goes on the feed." It's an unusual procedure, but undoubtedly sometimes works in an emergency. In the heavily fished, heavily populated stream where the fish refuses repeatedly and then takes, I'm assuming you're presenting a fly that closely resembles a natural the trout are taking and have finally presented it correctly.

There are a couple of specialized casts that can aid the attempt to show a fly to a fish before he sees any other sign of fisherman or tackle. You'll hear a great deal about throwing curves in dry-fly and nymph fishing, especially the former. A "curve" is for the purpose of keeping the leader away from the fish while providing enough slack for a little drag-free float. If you throw the fly on a perfectly straight leader, the drift is frequently abbreviated. Although nearly all dry-fly fishermen throw slack line from time to time, there are some good ones who never consciously throw true curve casts.

If a right-handed caster is standing to the right of and behind a fish facing upstream, he might want to throw a curve to the left, and that's the easiest one to do. He simply sideswipes a little so that his line is unrolling fairly parallel to the water, and he throws a bit harder than is necessary for the distance. So the leader goes a little past the fish, is snubbed up short as it straightens and whips around to the left. If properly delivered, the cast "dies" just above the water and the leader lands in a neat curve, with the fly then drifting down toward the fish.

For me, that's much easier than the curve to the right, which is generally executed in a similar sideswipe but with the cast allowed to die before the leader straightens out, thus dropping in a hook to the caster's right. This is touchier, in my estimation, because it's possible to spill your leader in a heap if you overdo it. Some fishermen deliver the curve to the right with a backhand motion, which can work for short distances. In any event, these fancy moves don't work very consistently with a great deal of line out. And wind is a big factor.

I believe many fishermen make the mistake of attempting too long a drag-free float, believing that the farther the fly drifts without moving unnaturally the better is the chance of its being taken. In fact, however, the farther it floats the more likely it is to be whipped by vagaries of current and the more likely there is to be excessive slack line. If the cast is long enough to give an extremely long float, such as 20 or 30 feet, it will have been thrown a long way past some of the fish that are expected to take it while leaving more chance for foul-ups of one kind or another. Some very good fishermen feel that it's better to show a fly to the fish only long enough to give him a chance to rise. That, of course, is when they are casting to rising trout or to specific spots they're pretty certain contain fish.

As implied earlier, a cardinal sin in covering water is to make an extra-long cast that bypasses water you intend to fish on succeeding throws—in other words, working your line over fish you hope to fool a little later. But once your fly has passed the optimum spot, if it continues to float undisturbed, so much the better. There is little danger of letting it go too far downstream.

Sunshine and shadow are important factors for the stream tactician to consider, and if my comments sound rather vague, it is because flat statements on this subject too are usually misleading. An overcast day produces the best fishing on many streams, and fishermen will tell you that it's because visibility isn't good and the fish are more easily fooled. That's true only part of the time. Ignoring the fact that certain insect hatches occur in cloudy or sunny weather, the water conditions, sun angle and stream surroundings must be considered in the light of visibility of the fisherman and his flies.

Actually fishing in situations in which you throw a moving shadow across the fish will probably turn them off, but it's also possible to get very close to fish if you stay in the sun's glare; I have seen fish very easy to catch when it was obvious they were looking almost at the sun as they rose to a dry fly. Undoubtedly, the fly's details were not clear and it was impossible for them to tell it from the real thing, whereas on a cloudy-bright day they might have been able to study it minutely.

When there are bushes or trees on the shady side of a river, it's often possible to stay in shadow and cast into sunny waters. Trout will lose interest in a man who stands perfectly still in the water for considerable time, though his casting motions may spook them anew. At some angles, difficult for a fisherman to figure, a rod tip and line high in the air may give off gleams that will put down a hundred trout. In light that's tough, the ancient and oft-quoted adage of "fishing fine and far off" is about all I can recommend. A low silhouette does no harm, although not everybody crouches as he fishes.

There's such a thing as sneaking up on a brook, taking advantage of bushes or trees and kneeling or actually lying on the bank to do the casting. I've had considerable success standing below beaver dams and fishing up into the ponds themselves, with only the top of my head higher than the dam.

Neutral clothing is a decided aid in trout fishing, and white hats or shirts are needless handicaps, regardless of the light. I don't think it makes much difference most of the time, but even a highly polished or brightly colored rod can cause trouble on occasions; a pure white rod can be a measurable disadvantage. One rabid believer in the cautious approach has all of his bamboo rods painted a neutral gray to match sky and scenery. Most fishermen would consider them disfigured.

With all my high-flown comments on dead drifts, judicious manipulation of surface flies to make them flutter a bit and the twitching of nymphs to make them swim, I still must subscribe to

Subdued clothing and a cautious approach are necessary on clear and heavily fished limestone streams. The angler is Harry Murray.

the deadliness of the simple downstream swing for some wet-fly conditions. Cast a wet fly across the current and let it swing down and across against a taut line, and it resembles nothing that lives or ever did as far as I know. What the trout, steelhead or Atlantic salmon think the thing is doing I can't imagine, but they hit it. At one point in its travel the swinging fly goes very fast and then it slows again, to hang below the fisherman if he's wading. Not only are fish likely to knock hell out of the thing, but there are certain parts of the swing they prefer under specific circumstances. If you are fishing for big brown trout in late fall, using large streamers, when you cast almost straight across the flow you seem most likely to get a strike just as the fly begins its fast cross-stream rush, and then again as it slows after crossing the current and is nearly straight downstream from the rod tip. Sometimes the fish follow through the fastest part of the swing and then strike at the slow-down. Since I know of no minnow that follows this procedure, I don't know why, but the swing triggers strikes.

The most common method of fishing for fresh-run Atlantic salmon is even more baffling, because the salmon isn't supposed to feed on its spawning run and at no time in its life has it ever fed on anything that looks like a salmon fly crossing a river. So here we have an unnatural situation that, nevertheless, sometimes requires the most meticulous attention to detail.

I must say a bit more about this Atlantic salmon thing, for there is no other fishing quite like it. Salmon fishing is done in the rivers as the fish are moving upstream to spawn or are pausing, resting or "holding" while on the way. Before they go to sea the small salmon feed on insect life, but once they take to salt water their primary food is small fishes, and it's doubtful if they ever take an insect during their years at sea. When they come back to the home stream and start up it they are not supposed to feed, yet they will strike a fly or lure now and then. The most popular wet flies used for salmon represent neither natural insects nor natural baitfish. They're pretty small, considering the size of fish expected, and are fished somewhat like streamers.

In most salmon waters the wet fly is simply cast across and slightly downstream and allowed to swing around with the current without manipulation of any kind, but the swing must be just so to catch fish. "Just so" is hard to describe, since you don't know what the fly is supposed to imitate. Sometimes it is desirable for the fly to be so near the surface that it causes a little wake, and sometimes a fisherman takes a half-hitch with his leader around the shank of the hook to encourage a riffle. When salmon are hard to come by, the position from which the fly is cast is extremely important, so the way you wade can count for a great deal. As in the case of trout, some of the best salmon anglers are not good casters, and some of the finest casters can go fishless because they aren't getting the fly to perform just right. Thus while the salmon is often rated as the king of all game fishes, the angling itself is a knack that sometimes has little similarity to other fishing techniques.

The "broadside float" is a principle that can be applied in both trout and salmon fishing and I ought to touch on it, even though it's hardly indispensable. The idea is to "mend" your line, flipping a section of it upstream after the wet fly is in the water, in order to cause the fly or streamer to come downstream crosswise of the current. Thus, as it drifts down toward the fish he can see it broadside and theoretically admire all the niceties of its construction. Otherwise, the fly is facing upstream and the fish is below it, thus getting only a stern view. Exponents of the broadside float also explain that when a fish takes a broadside fly it is natural for the fisherman to set the hook in a corner of its mouth, rather than pulling it straight forward, where it's more likely to come out.

This works in some fishing conditions, but I reiterate that sometimes it is the "swing" effect rather than a natural dead drift that fish, especially salmon, want. Before my first salmon-fishing trip I did considerable reading on the subject and approached the river with a box of expensive flies, light leaders and a firm conviction that the broadside drift would get me more than my share of salmon among peasants who evidently hadn't heard of it. My guide, who used something like 30-pound-test leader and very simple flies, thought my line mending was simply a casting problem of some sort and tried to help me overcome it. He continued to catch salmon and I didn't until it finally dawned on me that in that river at that time, the fish wanted the fly swinging downstream on a taut line in the simplest possible way—but just so.

There are many levels of apprehension a fish can experience when he sees a fisherman or becomes aware of his activities. Most anglers have observed some of the reactions of trout when they were in plain sight. When fish dart away in streaks, of course, you've generally had it for the time being at least, although I have seen brown trout return to their feeding stations no more than 10 minutes after a period of complete panic.

More subtle is the situation in which the fish simply stop feeding, generally dropping to the bottom and keeping quiet while the fisherman or his equipment remains in view. A lot of casts have been wasted over such fish because the angler thinks that as long as they don't leave, they're still likely to take. Most often this is wishful thinking, even though fish that live in water which is constantly bombarded by fishermen still have to eat *sometime* and, as noted earlier, will rise even while looking at fishermen. It's also true that Atlantic salmon often show no fear of waders or boaters as long as they are not being cut off from deep water, their natural sanctuary. But I want to emphasize that a fish can be well aware of a fisherman even though it does not flee the area.

I fish frequently in a section of water about 2 feet deep where the bottom is fairly smooth and the current gentle, and afternoon light will nearly always show at least a dozen rainbow trout in a 50-foot stretch. Most of them are about a foot long. There's no way of fishing the place without wading into it, and when I do that the fish always dart away; yet within 2 minutes of the time I stop moving, they begin to drop back to their former holding places near the bottom. They show no fear of me and may continue to feed guardedly on natural flies or nymphs, but I have never been able to hook one within 20 feet of my waders. If I make a cast of 50 feet or so, I'm likely to be in business. My point is that the fish watching me may be calm, but they are on guard and I can't fool them under the circumstances.

A splashy hooked fish sometimes puts the others down for a while, but in deep and turbulent water it's possible to catch literally dozens of trout from the same spot in a matter of minutes. It's a matter of a number of fish grouped at an ideal feeding spot, and they simply take their turns on the artificial flies the way they do on the naturals. So sometimes a hooked fish scares the others and sometimes it doesn't.

There's more than one way for a trout to hide, and in mud-bottomed pools with no other concealment I've often watched small brook trout "dig in" when they were alarmed. There would be a boil of mud for each fish, which would virtually disappear into its diggings. Once it was dug in, the trout would be almost impossible to see, even when you knew where it was.

We have to conclude that fish (like fishermen) are individualists, and in no area does this show more plainly than in their reactions to hookings. Trout fishermen who are personally acquainted with every outsized fish in their chosen waters tell of catching and releasing the same fish repeatedly, but most of them agree it's likely to be a few days before the victim is ready to take another chance. Being broken off from a light tippet evidently isn't too harrowing an experience, especially if a fish isn't played long before it happens. Fred

Terwilliger, who fishes western spring creeks, tells of breaking off the same fish twice within a 2-hour period and then landing it on the third try, thus recovering his flies from the fish's mouth. It was a sizable wild trout with a persistent preference for the exact same spot for feeding. Admittedly, a quick break-off from a light tippet is probably no more than a brief tug for the fish.

Grayling, which are not noted for intellect anyway, have been known to take a lure or fly immediately after being landed and released. Some of them are said to do it as many as four or five times, returning to the same "starting place" after each battle and becoming gradually weaker as the engagements wear on. That's unusual, of course, and one fish's behavior shouldn't be accepted as typical of an entire species.

7

AFTER IT'S CAUGHT

Since the subject of why, when and how you should release your catch has already been discussed, the time has now come to consider the other alternatives, and touch on what happens if you have decided to keep the fish. Most fish keepers have one of three things in mind—eating it, giving it away or having it mounted as a trophy—and this chapter will concern itself with these activities and their necessary preliminaries more or less in order.

Much of the angling literature implies that anyone not entranced by the taste of fresh trout is either deficient in some basic body chemistry or possessed of crude sensibilities in general. Maybe so, but I have long wondered why an ardent trout angler should necessarily love trout at the table unless that's the reason he got into the sport to begin with. The fact is, I know quite a number of top trout fishermen who don't care much for any seafood, while there are other heretics who spend all of their spare time fishing for trout yet confess in confidence that they prefer other kinds of fish at dinnertime. Finally, there are those who are so fond of trout in the stream or on the line that they are against all trout cookery.

Flat statements to the effect that all brook trout are exceptionally tasty or that no hatchery rainbows are fit to eat should be regarded with suspicion. There are too many variables involved. To begin with, a fish is the product of what it eats, and human diners too are strongly influenced by their current environment. A healthy trout with a good choice of food in water of the right temperature and purity is likely to be good at the table (provided, of course, that it's been properly cared for between stream and stove). Furthermore, a cold, wet and half-starved camping fisherman in primitive country will sometimes wax ecstatic over a fish dish he'd turn up his nose at in a fancy restaurant.

Beyond these factors, there's more difference in the quality of individual trout than is usually recognized. I think the best trout I ever ate was a 3½-pound brown, cut up and fried in butter shortly after it struck a large dry fly. As it happens, I am one of those anglers who are not overly fond of fish, while another of us who ate that trout on that day did it simply because there was nothing else. He hated fish—made a point of it, and in fact searched fruitlessly for something else while the fish was cooking. (This wasn't really a camping trip; we'd simply been caught out with simple cooking equipment and had to make out as best we could.)

Well, anyway, the fish was superb. Its flesh was pinker than that of any other trout we'd caught in the same place, and all three of us who dined on that brown agreed it was the best fish we'd ever tasted.

In fact, the fish hater was so impressed that he meticulously checked the campfire, the skillet and the amount of butter used and 2 days later tried to duplicate the performance. This time it came out just fish. My wife and I were the other two anglers involved, and we also tried to get the same result again, using another big brown trout over a fire made on the very same rocks. We were properly hungry and the meal was good, but not really as good as the first one. My only explanation is that the first trout had been eating just the right things.

The addition of elaborate seasoning to fish is considered disgraceful by those who feel that nothing can improve the natural taste of fish, but my advice is, if you have to disguise a fish, do it. It's better than throwing the fish away, and a "fishy" taste doesn't please everybody.

Of course, if the fish is really rank, there's something wrong. In other words, it's a long way from freshly caught fish to really rank fish, and most of what you eat is somewhere in between. The fish's digestive chemicals begin to work on the fish itself after it is killed, and this both contributes to spoilage and can change the taste of a fish that isn't truly "spoiled." Thus after a fish is killed it should be cleaned as soon as possible and kept as cool as possible. Oily fish are most likely to spoil. Of the fish we're dealing with, some of the Pacific salmon have the most oil, and the king salmon is noted for it.

Stringers are used by boat fishermen, and sometimes by waders, as a means of keeping fish alive longer, but in most trout country the angler is into and out of the water so much the fish are dead before long anyway, for the trouts aren't the best livers on stringers. Snap stringers are much better than those which go through the gills, but stringed fish get banged around a great deal and the flesh is bruised. When a fish dies on a stringer, it's best to take it off and get it out of the water immediately.

Boats with live wells sometimes keep fish lively for considerable periods. Fish can also be kept alive in the water with a wire basket made for the purpose, or even when left in a mesh bag, seldom seen anymore.

The humane way of dealing with a trout that is to be eaten is to kill it by hitting it on the head before putting it into any creel. Small ones can be banged against a rock. With big ones it's easier to bang the rock against the fish, and a fist-sized stone is about right. A stick or the back of a fish knife works fine. A "priest" is a club sometimes carried by fishermen for dealing with larger fish, and this is very convenient, although one more thing to carry. Some fishing knives have a weighted part designed specially for the purpose of dispatching the catch.

As noted earlier, the traditional conveyance for a wading fisherman's trout used to be the wicker creel, but good ones are now hard to get and very expensive, and their use is declining fast. Nonetheless, the principles of the creel are good. It provides shade, permits ventilation and keeps the fish away from the fisherman's body heat.

Canvas creels being put to use on Montana's Madison River. With the water a bit too cloudy for flies, these anglers turned to spinning tackle and spoons, which proved to be the answer for this big brown trout.

The canvas creel shares some of these advantages while being inexpensive and compact, to boot. The canvas creel is designed to cool its contents through an evaporation process, like a desert water bag, while the fish itself is kept dry in a plastic liner. Some users of wicker creels maintain that they should be immersed at intervals to keep the fish damp, though all agree that a dead fish shouldn't be kept underwater. However, most fishermen simply ignore the dampness business.

FIELD DRESSING

There are several ways of getting the innards out of a trout, and the obvious one is to slit from the vent to the lower jaw with a sharp knife and simply remove the viscera by hand.

Filleting does not require that the viscera be removed. Lay the fish on its side and make a cut crosswise just back of the gills and pectoral fin. Slice the flesh away from the rib cage by working the knife along the backbone, and then push the blade all the way through the fish from back to belly and cut toward the tail. The fillet will be cut free at the tail. Then do the same on the other side.

When a fish is field-dressed, the strip of blood along the backbone (it's the fish's kidney) should be removed. In most trout you can do this easily by running a thumb along the spine inside the body cavity. With really large fish, you may have to use a knife to get started. The gills should be removed, even when the head is left on.

I am told a fish will be better to eat if killed immediately rather than allowed to die of suffocation out of water, but tons of commercially caught fish are allowed to die in iced holds or heaped on a deck.

Trout keep better in chipped ice than on large blocks of it, but excess water should be drained off. Snow is used for efficient storage by many high-country fishermen. When frozen for considerable periods, fish should be wrapped so that there will be no air pockets to cause frost inside the wrapper and produce freezer burn. Fillets or whole smaller fish are best kept if placed in milk cartons, which are then filled with water and frozen solid.

The best method of storing a fish far from ice evokes disagree-

After removing viscera from a trout at streamside, the fisherman uses his thumb to clean out the streak of blood along the fish's spine.

ment. The descriptions of colorful trout lying in a basket on a bed of ferns or willow twigs are undoubtedly more poetic, but believers in dry storage forgo such colorful packing, saying that greenery gets hot and that dried grass or hay is much better.

In a dry climate, cleaned trout can be treated with a little salt and pepper (equal parts) rubbed along the spine, and hung in the shade until they are thoroughly dried. They will keep for several days that way. When it's time to cook them, they lose their dried-out appearance if soaked in cold water for half an hour and can be cooked as if freshly caught.

THE COOKING

This isn't a cookbook, but a few recipes can get you started. Camp cookery can go from subsistence fare to gourmet stuff. I guess my best-remembered fish dinner was eaten on the Pine River in British Columbia. I was alone, had a crude camp and was fishing for grayling. Late in the evening I caught a large grayling, started for camp already chilled and got in over my hip boots in some very cold water. I got a big fire going (more to get warm by than for cooking), split the grayling down the belly, opened the body and mounted it on a forked willow stick, hurriedly threading the prongs through the flesh. Then I propped the stick so that the inside of the fish's body would be exposed to the flames and busied myself by filling my wet boots with warm pebbles to dry them out.

The grayling cooked faster than I expected and fell off the dingle stick into the ashes, but I retrieved it and ate one of the finest fish dinners I can recall. As I finished picking the bones I smelled rubber burning and found that the pebbles I'd put into my boots were too hot. They'd burned holes—but I was warm and full and crawled happily into my sleeping bag.

Frying

Fancy Continental chefs consider boiled trout ("au bleu") a great delicacy, I'm told, but most American trout end up either fried, sautéed or broiled. No elaborate advance preparation is required. Trout scales are very small and can be rubbed off. Some cooks pay no attention to them at all. Very small trout are generally fried in oil with the fins left on and the bones left in. If thoroughly cooked the small bones can be eaten, but the diner can strip the flesh from them with little difficulty. Many larger trout are filleted. Salmon and large trout are often cut crosswise, or "steaked," for cooking. A good steak thickness is an inch or slightly less.

Simple fish frying is done efficiently with about an inch of cooking oil or shortening in a skillet over a medium fire. Before the small fish or pieces of larger trout are added to the oil they are generally rolled in dry flour with salt, pepper and any other seasoning added. Most cooks turn them once for a total of about 8 minutes' cooking time. The outsides should be crisp. The oil should be what cooks call "medium hot" before the fish are added.

Sautéed, or pan-fried, fish employ only two or three spoonfuls of shortening over a medium-low heat, and the fish or fillets should be dry before being placed in the skillet. When fried fish is done it will flake slightly when tested with a fork. A variety of breading ingredients are used on pan-fried fish, including flour, cracker or bread crumbs or cornmeal, but none is absolutely necessary.

Broiling and Grilling

Fish of any size may be broiled. If you're dealing with steaks of salmon, steelhead or other large specimens, they can be about an inch think. For a pair of them use ¼ cup of salad oil, juice from one lemon and ½ teaspoonful of salt, of which you apply a small amount to the pieces before cooking begins. The broiler should be preheated about 10 minutes, and cooking should take about 3 minutes on each side, the rest of the lemon, oil and salt applied by basting with a brush. Of course, other seasoning can be added. One simple broiling procedure involves a simple mixture of mayonnaise, salt and pepper spread over fillets.

Grilling is about the same as broiling except that the fire is underneath the fish. As with broiling, the cooking grill should be preheated to avoid sticking.

Foil Cooking

Campfire cooking with aluminum foil has had years of publicity, is simple and takes a minimum of equipment. It works fine on fish. You simply clean the trout and wrap it in a sheet of foil with oil or butter, salt and pepper, allow a wood fire to burn down to hot coals and place the package in the coals. Roasting 4 minutes on each side will take care of most packages. If the pieces are especially thick, the cooking time must be slightly extended.

Smoking

Smoking trout is simplified by the small units now available at moderate price, and smoked salmon is a delicacy of long reputation. For quantity operations, homemade smokers are often built from old refrigerators, but few fishermen want to do that much of it. Smoked fish keeps well for several days after preparation. If there's a warning to be given here, it's that no matter how good smoked fish may be, most people tire rather quickly of a steady diet of it.

Baking

Very large trout or salmon, whatever the kind, are supposed to lack the delicate flavor of smaller ones. There are fishermen who want to eat only small fish of less than half a pound, and others say the quality of a brown trout, for example, begins to fall off in fish of more than 2 pounds—but some folks simply don't see much difference. Big trout are frequently baked whole after dressing and are usually stuffed.

A typical recipe for a 4-pounder would include ½ teaspoon of salt, 1½ teaspoons of butter or margarine, 2 cups of chopped mushrooms, a cup of bread crumbs and some powdered rosemary. A little water, milk or white wine is added. The fish is prepared with its head on or off, and the cavity is rubbed with lemon juice and dusted with salt and pepper. When the stuffing is installed, the fish may be closed by skewers and sewing. It's cooked for around 40 minutes in an oven that's been preheated to 350 degrees.

Remember that all cooking takes more time at high altitude, and much trout country is high.

DEAD GIVEAWAY

Years ago when there was a fairly surefire public fishing center at Fishing Bridge in Yellowstone National Park, observers found that it simply isn't in the nature of the average tourist fisherman to return any fish to the water once he's caught it. The joys of possession were so great that an occasional fisherman simply couldn't part with his catch, even though he had no real intention of cooking it. The park garbage cans claimed a large share of the catch in those days, and those who dumped those thousands of cutthroat trout couldn't really explain why they'd kept them in the first place; mankind is just that kind of creature.

Strangely, a few veteran fishermen have not outgrown the fish-keeping habit and even when they don't want them feel they must take home what they catch. Many fish are given away to other people who don't want them, and I know a popular politician who receives regular gifts of uncleaned fish at odd hours. He doesn't care for fish but has extremely fast-growing rosebushes.

I'd guess a large percentage of fish that are given away are wasted. If you want to make a present of fresh trout, clean them carefully and be sure the recipient really wants them. Unless there's a prior agreement, I'm afraid a present of uncleaned fish late at night wins few friends.

TAXIDERMY

Every fisherman I know seems to be a voluble critic of taxidermy, able to hold forth at length on any specimen shown to him. In fact, unless the fish can still swim it is bound to draw disparaging remarks, and a taxidermist must either become callused to such criticism or avoid confrontation by critics.

Coloring comes in for many complaints, though there's so much difference in trout coloration that even a fisheries biologist will generally refuse to identify one by its color. The taxidermist may have a complete set of color charts for every trout known to man and may work from innumerable color photographs, but even trout on the same fly from the same pool on the same day are often startlingly different in hue. If you want a fish to look the way it appeared when it came from the water you'd better take a color photo immediately, which you probably won't do. Within a few minutes the fish will look different.

I once made a series of pictures of a very large steelhead, moving it to three different settings a considerable distance apart. The process took about three hours and although the fish looked good at each stop, the finished transparencies appeared to have been made from three different fish. And now you have an idea of what the taxidermist is confronted with. It's not at all unusual for a client to take a fish back to have it painted differently because his fish was "more silvery" or "more reddish," or lighter or darker, than the standard color put on by the taxidermist.

A job of taxidermy, from the fisherman's viewpoint, is almost always an emergency. He usually hasn't thought about what he'd do if he caught a fish big enough to deserve being mounted, and not many anglers have very many fish preserved. In choosing a taxidermist I'd prefer one who operates in or near trout country and specializes in local trout, for a sailfish specialist may not be too

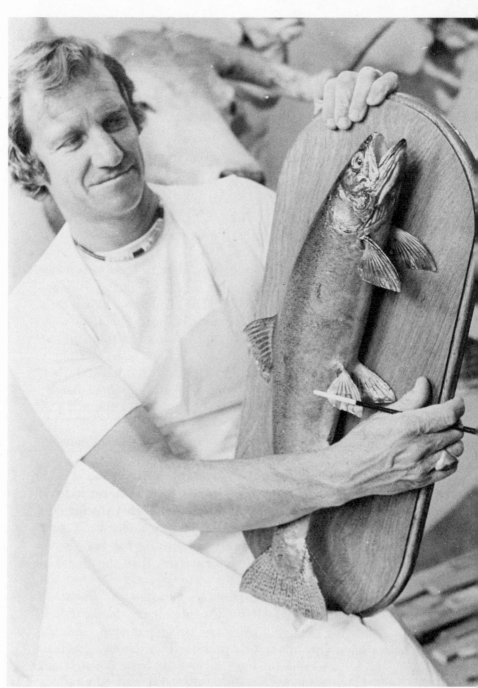

True trout taxidermy involves skinning the fish and then placing the skin over a form, after which the proper colors are added. Taxidermists who specialize in trout should be sought whenever possible. This is Dean Jehowski of Lentfer's Taxidermy Studio, Livingston, Montana.

experienced with cutthroats. Now, although you shouldn't be bashful about your own preference, you'd be wise to choose a type of mount recommended by the man who's going to set it up, and he'll probably give you a choice of several kinds. The most frightening mess I've seen resulted when I told a taxidermist how to do a fish in a way he'd never tried before. He didn't want to do it, but I insisted. Eventually I paid my bill and threw the mount into the trash.

"Taxidermy" is a loosely used term, because some mounts are simply painted castings. Others employ the complete skin of the fish and use the original fins. Even when the "real" fish doesn't look quite as good as a more artificial mount, it may mean more to the person who caught it. I have heard a great number of fishermen say wistfully that they weren't sure the fish they got back was the fish they had caught, and some of them have launched full-scale investigations.

When a fish's skin is used, the fish's body is employed in making a mold; then a casting is made and the fish's skin sewed over the prepared body. The fins are carded and dried and then backed up with plastic.

It is much easier to make a casting of a fish—the method is detailed in Al McClane's *New Standard Fishing Encyclopedia*—and paint it to suit. Even some nonprofessionals make their own.

One substitute for taxidermy is a simple outline of a catch made on a board and painted to suit. If the painting is primitive, some like it that much better, as it would be very difficult to get the colors exact. Such fish "plaques" hang in some very expensive dens.

When you catch a fish you want to have skinned by a taxidermist, handle it as little as possible. Don't clean it unless you're stuck a long way from the freezing equipment. If you have to remove the viscera, do it with an incision in the less attractive side and remember there'll be a "display" side that should keep its scales intact. If the fish is frozen, do it on a board. Be especially careful of the fins on the display side.

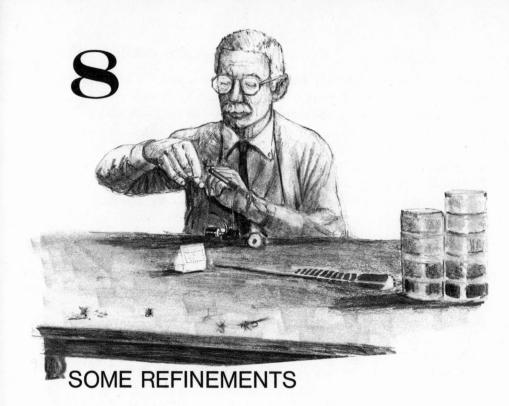

8

SOME REFINEMENTS

There is hardly an aspect of trout fishing that cannot be pursued to great depth through reading, observation and experimentation, yet many obscure technical matters and some quite basic ones can be largely ignored, if you choose, in a long and successful career of angling. This chapter will deal with a few of the more specialized subjects, and our purpose is mainly to introduce you to them; even if you never need to apply them to your own fishing, it's often nice to have an idea of what others are referring to. Hence this chapter will be something of a catchall, and its topics are not necessarily closely related.

RISE FORMS

"Rise forms" are simply the ways in which trout takes flies, for although there are some waters where a trout is never seen until it is hooked, there are many others where the feeding can be observed. "Fishing the rise" is simply casting to fish that are feeding on or near to the surface so that they make a visible disturbance. The problem becomes what they are taking, and this isn't quite as easy as you'd think. Rise forms have been rigidly catalogued by writers on the trout subject, and some of them have been given descriptive names.

The easiest one to recognize is a matter of a trout's taking an insect that's large enough to be visible to the fisherman and which is a truly dry fly, floating high. Sometimes such rises are fairly noisy, generally heard as a distinct "slurp" or "glub." The trout simply rises up from its feeding station, opens its mouth, allows the fly to enter and sinks again. Big trout are likely to make less disturbance than small ones, simply because their mouths are sufficiently large for capturing the fly to be no big project. Then too, the big fish simply isn't addicted to quick and violent rushes for so small a morsel. A very small trout may rise splashily, even to a small fly, for he has a small mouth to catch it with, and for him it's a pretty important trip. Nevertheless, when you watch a big fish operate for a while he's likely to reveal his size by a broad swirl or an important gurgle, even if he never gets too excited.

When you actually see a natural fly disappear in the fish's mouth you certainly know what's going on, but there are still some pitfalls. The worst occurs when the rising fish are feeding on a particular kind of insect at a time when another insect is more plentiful. It's easy to jump to the conclusion that the desired fly is the one that's appearing in the greatest numbers. There are also occasions when fish that choose a particular insect today switch to another kind tomorrow, even though both have been hatching at the same time. The most learned trout student cannot explain this, which is a sort of peak in the business of selectivity. Sometimes binoculars are helpful in figuring it out.

At least, when you see flies disappear you can be certain of what you're trying to imitate. At the beginning of my trout career I assumed that any time a trout splashed, swirled or made a surface ring it was taking a dry fly, and I will never forget standing beside a pool that was almost boiling with big trout and casting until my arm hurt without result; I was using a dry fly and the fish were taking nymphs just beneath the surface.

One of the most confusing rises is the "dimple," which is just that—a fish taking very quietly and leaving only a silent ring on smooth water. The first impression is that only a small fish could have made so slight a disturbance, and to make it worse, a fingerling is quite capable of it. However, a large trout can also make a dimple with the gentle sucking motion of drawing down an insect. Very small food items, barely afloat, can provoke dimpling, and some tiny artificials that serve in such situations are what I call "film flies"— not riding high like the conventional dry but not sinking either. Sometimes you can't catch dimplers, but I have experienced some of my best fishing when only the silent circle marked a trout's rise.

The "head-and-tail" rise involves a fish showing its head, back and tail as it goes over and down, often quite slowly. This is very common when the fish is taking something just under the surface, although it is sometimes used also on a high-floating dry.

Another movement that can be taken for a surface rise is a swirl caused by the fish's tail when it is actually grubbing on the bottom in shallow water. Of course, it isn't a rise at all, and anything that might get that fish's attention would probably have to be within an inch of the bottom.

LEADERS

As mentioned in Chapter 3, you'll probably prefer to buy ready-made leaders to begin with, but later you'll probably want to make up your own.

In nearly all fly fishing you'll need tapered leaders, for they improve your casting and can deliver a more delicate fly. Most experienced fishermen make up the tapers by knotting together pieces of monofilament of the right size. The knots do no harm; in fact, they help to turn the cast over. The large end, or butt section, of the leader is permanently attached to the fly line and is likely to be used all season while the other extreme, the tippet, may be replaced several times a day.

You can cast a longer leader than you think if it's properly tapered, and some fishermen actually use leaders more than 20 feet long when fishing small flies on flat water. Employing more than 15 feet of leader with an average rod becomes a bit awkward, espe-

Spools of leader material are most convenient when strung on chains or cords for storage in vest.

cially when you're making a short cast. It's also an inconvenience when you play a fish, as the knots are continually moved through the guides. In most trout fishing a leader slightly longer than the rod is sufficient, and I've never used anything longer than 15 feet except to experiment. In broken water a 9-foot leader is satisfactory, and very short leaders are often used with sinking lines to hold a buoyant fly close to the bottom. Even a wet fly can be whipped off the bottom by strong currents unless it is hitched close to the heavy line.

You can buy ready-made leaders that are tied up in sections, or you can get "drawn" monofilament in a knotless taper. The objection to the latter is that if you want to replace the small end, make it smaller or larger or adjust the leader's length, you still have to tie on another piece sooner or later. Don't be afraid of splicing knots in a leader; the best of fishermen use them.

Under some circumstances you'll actually dress your leaders with a solution to make them float, especially with small nymphs fished near the surface, as a twitch of the floating leader may be the only sign of a strike you'll have. In other cases you'll want the leader to sink; but I don't think it's generally important in dry-fly fishing whether it floats or not. Unless it goes down so quickly it yanks a small fly under, I wouldn't worry too much about it. It's one of those endless arguments, some saying a floating leader is too visible and others believing a sunken one resembles a hawser from the fish's viewpoint. Light makes the difference. There's no doubt that any-thing but the very finest leader is visible, floating or sinking, to a trout if his attention is attracted to it, but if he takes a fly, he just hasn't noticed.

Monofilament is measured by the pull it takes to break it and also by its diameter. Fly fishermen use an "X rating" in classifying leader size, a carry-over from the days when leaders were made up of silkworm gut. The larger the number of the rating, the smaller the diameter of the material. A very coarse leader end would be 0X, and a very small tippet would be 7X.

Spin fishermen or bait casters class their lines by pound test, and the diameters of various synthetic materials vary greatly for a given strength. This table shows the X ratings of monofilament leader material with the measurements in thousandths of an inch and the approximate pound tests, which vary considerably.

0X	.011"	9 lbs.
1X	.010"	7.8 lbs.
2X	.009"	7 lbs.
3X	.008"	5.3 lbs.
4X	.007"	3.5 lbs.
5X	.006"	2.5 lbs.
6X	.005"	1.8 lbs.
7X	.004"	1 lb.

In a fairly swift "freestone" river, you might do just as well with 6-pound-test tippets as with anything smaller. When you fish slow-moving waters with highly sophisticated trout, the tippet size becomes critical and even dramatic. I have fished small dry flies with 5X leaders amid trout wallowing like porpoises and received no attention for my pains, then changed to a 6X tippet and hooked fish after fish on the same fly. The latter size—6X—is generally about as small as the average angler can handle consistently, and even then, since the test of his unknotted leader is less than 2 pounds, he'll break off some fish in setting the hook; but of course, it's used every day of trout season and accounts for many large catches. When there's vegetation or other underwater obstacles, it's hard to hold a fish of more than 2 pounds on such fine material. When you go to 7X, your reflexes must be just right and your rod tip should match the threadlike mono. Personally, I find 7X about as fine as I can handle, and although I hear other fishermen tell of even finer leaders, I don't recall ever seeing a trout of more than 2 pounds being landed on 7X. My point is that it's difficult and not common, so don't start having feelings of inferiority.

More careful casting can often take the place of ultralight tippets. There was the sad but enlightening day when I tried 5X tippets and did very poorly, then went to 6X and began to catch fish. I watched another fisherman doing quite well and learned he was casting 5X and "never used anything smaller." He simply delivered his fly with more care. Smarting with humiliation, I went back to 5X, found a corpulent brown trout rising regularly and told myself he could be caught if I'd use enough care. I waded carefully, took up a good position, fed him my No. 18 Light Cahill just right and watched him gulp it. Then I did the same thing several more times. I'd been using an ultralight tippet to make up for sloppy casting.

The bad news in this is that the inexperienced or heavy-handed fisherman, the fellow most likely to break off a fish with light terminal gear, is also the one who may need very fine leaders to get a rise at all. The careful expert, who could probably handle fish on a very fine tippet, sometimes gets by without it by using a good approach and careful presentation.

A fine tippet is hard to slap down on the water and may deliver a fly daintily, even with awkward casting. A reasonably light tippet helps in two ways—causing the fly to alight delicately and being less noticeable to the fish. Very light tippets are hard to fish in high winds, but there's less need for them when wind is riffling the water.

Hook setting should consist of a quick lift of the rod tip, as distinguished from a jerk. A hard jerk will cause the rod tip to bow toward the fish a split second before it springs back the other way, and many a fisherman who thinks he must jerk harder to hook more of his strikes is making things worse as he goes along. And whether it's the fisherman or the fish that delivers a quick tug, a break-off can occur so easily that you wonder what happened. In tests with scales and heavy rods I find a man can jerk more than 10 times as hard as he pulls steadily. It takes one hell of a wrist to snap a 2-pound leader when you're bending a long rod steadily at a right angle to the fish, but give it a little jerk and it's all over.

In tying up leaders, you want the butt section to be approximately two-thirds to three-fourths the size of the end of the fly line, and that usually comes to about 30-pound test. An ideally profiled leader is about 60 percent butt, 20 percent step-down and 20 percent tippet. A good 9-footer would have a butt with about 40 inches of around. 022, about 20 inches of about .016 and then three or four 6-inch sections to step it down to a 20-inch tippet of the size needed. I won't be too definite about the size of the step-down sections because the size of the tippet will have a bearing there. As long as they knot easily they're probably all right.

An example might start with a butt tapered to .016; the 6-inch step-downs might be 0X, 2X and 4X and the tippet might be 5X or 6X. You'll go out of your mind if you try to be too exact on this, but many fishermen are incredibly sloppy.

There are three reasons for keeping the tippet fairly long: the fly will turn over more lightly, the heavier section will be farther from the fish and there will be added stretch in the light stuff so it won't break so easily. You can go into the physics endlessly, but these basics are all you really need.

You can depart considerably from those measurements, but that gives you something to start with. Few casters are really careful with their leader measurements, most of them being unable to quote them to you.

A simple overhand knot in a piece of monofilament weakens it tremendously—more than you'd think; and the tighter the knot is drawn the easier it is to snap. Those accidental knots (everybody gets them occasionally) are called "wind knots"—a graceful cop-out, for they can appear when there's hardly a breeze. If you're doing tricky casting, there are a hundred ways of manufacturing one occasionally. Keep checking for them.

IMPRESSION VERSUS IMITATION

One of the oldest controversies in the fly-fishing business is the "imitation" fly as opposed to the "impression" fly. The exact-imitation school believes that the closer you can come to the living thing, the better are your chances of success. I can think of no human reason why this shouldn't be so; but fish have a disturbing habit of preferring something that gives only a general impression of food. Hardly any of the hundreds of spoons, spinners and plugs that take trout more than vaguely resemble a minnow or frog; biologists say they trigger strikes simply because the fish is used to feeding when it sees something that hurries, darts and flashes. Strangely, lures that have been built in the exact images of food fish have had very limited success, and the same thing is true of some "exact" flies.

Some of the outstanding examples of "impression" flies are large and gaudy and have not the slightest resemblance to any real insect. I believe the best-known fly in the world is the Royal Coachman, which serves both wet and dry and is simply an eye-pleasing combination of colors. The hair-winged Royal Coachman (same colors but with bushy hair wings instead of feather wings) departs even further from any living insect and is an especially popular dry pattern because it is so highly visible to the fisherman. It certainly isn't used to match any hatch, but it catches a great many fish when there is no visible activity at all.

Perhaps the extreme in an impression fly, however, is something like the Trude, a popular number, especially among some guides who use boats. The Trude has a nearly horizontal wing of feather or hair, a bit of a tail and some hackle (the part that represents legs on most dry flies). Ray Hurley, with whom it's a favorite, explained that it will serve as almost anything. As a boat drifts down the river the fisherman can lay his Trude lightly near the bank and as it floats downstream it resembles a grasshopper. Even when it is moved a little it might be a floating 'hopper. Then, if the current gets it and sweeps it under, it becomes a streamer of sorts, looking like a small baitfish. Anyway, it catches a great many fish.

It's much the same with the nymph. I recall one experiment in which a dedicated believer in realism actually made meticulous molds from the real thing and produced imitations you'd have to examine carefully to tell them from the original, but their success was limited and they were badly outscored by some fuzzy and shapeless little gadgets consisting of a few dabs of hair and thread. Some analysts have gone so far as to say that a fish becomes more critical if the thing is a nearly exact imitation and is more likely to take a vague fly of about the right size when there is no detail of which to be critical.

FLY DESIGN

In addition to the ordinary forms of dry flies, wet flies, nymphs and streamers there are countless special ways of constructing them, some of which are unusual enough to merit listing.

The conventional dry fly has stiff hackles, or "legs." (Hackles are generally the bristly parts of a feather that stand out when the "spine," or "quill," of the feather is wrapped around a hook or fly body.) In use, the hackles sit on the water and hold the main part of the fly, including the body; tail, or "tag," and wings away from the surface. A "no-hackle" fly, as detailed in the book *Selective Trout* by Doug Swisher and Carl Richards, uses no hackles at all, and the body of the fly rests on the water.

A "bivisible" fly is the opposite, having no wings and very little body and being made up almost entirely of hackle. A "hair-wing" fly uses hair instead of feathers for its wings. A "down-wing" type, which might represent a caddis or stone fly, has a wing or wings that go nearly straight back instead of upward. A "fan-wing" design has the wings well separated. "Spiders," or "skating spiders," are usually tied with long but sparse hackle "legs" and with a small hook riding in the center with the hook's eye up. A "spent-wing" pattern would

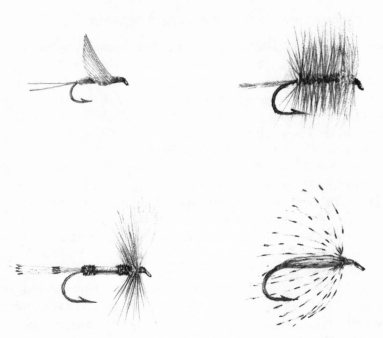

Specialized types of flies: top left, a no-hackle dry; top right, a bivisible; middle left, a hair-wing (Royal Coachman); middle right, a soft-hackle; bottom left, a Muddler; bottom right, a Woolly Worm. Creative fly tiers claim that half the fun comes from inventing your own patterns.

represent a fly that had died and had its wings nearly straight out from the body.

The midge fly deserves special mention. It's very small; one productive imitation is somewhere between dry and wet flies, for it represents the pupa of an immature insect which floats vertically with most of the body submerged. The imitation rides with the hook hanging down, a hook that may be No. 20 or smaller.

There are special dry flies such as grasshoppers or beetles which don't conform to conventional construction, but they are easily recognized. In some cases, cork-bodied bugs catch fish, but they are more popular for bass and sunfish than for trout.

The conventional wet fly may come in the same pattern as a dry except that its hackles are soft and fold back against the body when it is moved or held against the current.

A nymph, whether made of hair, feathers or other material, resembles an immature water insect in some stage of development. The Woolly Worm flies probably represent very large nymphs or drowned land creatures.

We should make special mention of the "flymph" and the "soft-hackle" flies. The "flymph," so-called by Vernon S. Hidy because it represents a nymph just as it rises to become a fly, is characterized by soft hackles that work in the water as it is fished, resembling a nymph squirming to escape its shuck. The "soft-hackle" fly as featured by author Sylvester Nemes (*The Soft-Hackled Fly*) has the same type of action in the water and, like the flymph, could be either an actively swimming nymph or one ready to shed its shuck.

The streamers, representing small fish for the most part, generally present a rather long silhouette and are streamlined in the water as well as in the air while being cast. There's a special group that has evolved from the Muddler Minnow, originally devised by Don Gapen of Nipigon, Ontario. It's distinguished by a large, bristly head made from deer hair and was originally made with a turkey-feather wing and tail and a tinsel-wrapped body, but there are literally hundreds of variations of all sizes. Many commercial fly manufacturers feature the Muddler in several forms. Dave Whitlock has several designs of his own, and Chester Marion, a Montana guide and master fisherman, uses dozens of variations he ties himself. The Muddler was originally intended to imitate the sculpin, or bullhead, but it has been used to catch fish of many kinds all over the world, many of which have never seen a sculpin.

It can serve as a grasshopper or large stone fly when floating and becomes the bullhead—or something else—when pulled under. Such fishing may lose something in esthetics, but it results in a great many fish. A. J. McClane has described the Muddler as "the most versatile and popular fly in this century."

Most of the flies used for Atlantic salmon are wets, and there has been a great change in them in recent years. Since Atlantic salmon fishing has been a highly traditional sport, the flies had followed suit and were highly ornamental, constructed from exotic feathers from the far reaches of the globe. Feathers were often laboriously "married" (interwoven) and very expensive. In more recent years, tiers have simplified the patterns, made them less expensive and often departed from the old names. They seem to catch just as many fish. Some very tiny dry flies have been used for salmon, but most dries are large, bushy patterns, frequently made up largely of hair.

Steelhead flies of the Pacific Coast and the Great Lakes are both streamers and more compact wet flies and are generally uncomplicated in construction. Some of them are simple ties of fluorescent yarn, originally intended to imitate salmon eggs, a favorite steelhead food.

HOMEMADE FLIES

A large percentage of trout fishermen tie their own flies, though there are very few who do not buy at least part of their supply. Learning how isn't all that difficult, and a selection of books on the subject is listed at the end of this book in Appendix A. For anyone who wants to make the tying a major part of the hobby, the materials can be almost endless and quite expensive. For fishermen who want to tie only those patterns they use a great deal on their favorite streams, the stock of materials can be simplified, and the ultimate savings are considerable.

Large streamers are easy to tie, and after them come the larger dries and wets. Nymphs are often quite simple, and some of the deep-fished steelhead flies are little more than wads of colorful yarn. It's the materials that can get expensive—the basic tools are not costly, and I'd recommend getting high quality to begin with, even if your tying activities are going to be limited. As in some other things, the beginner is the one who needs the best tools and is least likely to have them.

It's possible to buy kits containing everything needed to get started. For around the price of a good glass rod you get a good vise, bobbin, hackle pliers, whip finisher and scissors with an assortment of thread, tinsel, head cement, hooks, dubbing materials (fur and other things which can be rolled up into bodies), some hair and some gamecock necks.

You'll have no use for some of the things in the supply of feathers and will immediately want more of other items, as well as some hair or fur that isn't included, but the kit will contain the basics.

If you want to tie flies simply to keep from buying them, it may not be practical. However, if you really believe you'd enjoy making your own, you can enjoy some creative work and sometimes adapt to fishing situations that aren't handled by what you'd buy in a store. Then you can name your own creations and add your list to the thousands appearing in books on trout fishing. It'll keep you off the streets.

WADING

There are fishermen who can wade mysteriously through deep torrents over slippery bottoms and never get wet and others who continually fall in for no known reason. If you are going to do much stream fishing, the matter is worth some thought. A tall fisherman, of course, has some obvious advantages in wading. Coordination, a sense of balance and athletic ability can be helpful in some of the wilder waters, and being able to read the current is beneficial—but some otherwise ordinary mortals are peerless waders.

And although I may not be able to explain the best or the worst waders, I can give some practical advice, which begins with proper footwear, using felt or soft metal on the soles.

It's easy to get lulled into trouble. After prancing around through swift water with good footing, many an angler of short experience has walked nonchalantly into a stream that looked much like what he was used to, only to find himself floundering helplessly and trying to catch his valuables before they floated away. Since trout streams are cold, the shock of a fall-in can be considerable. For some absurd reason, a fall-in viewed by others is also humiliating, and I do not know whether laughter or sympathy makes me madder.

You begin with the assumption you are going to fall in, for you will eventually, and you should plan your equipment so that water won't harm it. If you wear eyeglasses, you should have them fastened to you—and it's a good idea for a fly caster to wear spectacles even if his vision is perfect.

With practice you'll learn to judge the quality of your footing, and the cardinal rule is to be sure one foot is solidly placed before moving the other. In tricky water the steps should be short, and you keep your narrowest silhouette to the current. Much of the time you'll just push one foot forward and then pull the other up to it.

You should try to set your feet so that you can push upstream, because once you begin to be forced downstream out of control, the chances are you're due to be laundered.

If you work your way into really tough wading, remember the route you have taken for the return trip. When groping for footholds, try to avoid the high places, for only by getting into the low spots will you be able to gauge the water's depth, and the footing will be better there anyway.

If you feel graceful and the water's not too cold, you can learn to dance for short distances through deep, fast water with the current

Paul Bruun wades in heavy, swift water to fish a big streamer for brown trout. He braces himself so that the current strikes from the side.

carrying you along and without solid footing. Some good waders do that when they have a definite objective to reach; but it takes fine balance, and the best of them get dunked sometimes. I have heard of the "daring" necessary for good wading. Let's make that "confidence." "Daring" may be fine except when the water is near freezing and it's a long way to a fire. Then it becomes damned foolishness.

A large proportion of wettings come from a form of panic. A fisherman hops and teeters around where he can barely stand and stays at it until his nerves begin to betray him. He decides to get out of the tricky spot, and with easy wading only a few feet away he lunges for it. Splud!

There's disagreement about the use of wading staffs, some believing the staff should be used upstream. That hasn't worked for me. I stick the foot of the staff slightly downstream to hold me against the current. There are folding and telescoping wading staffs, or you can pick up a stick in an emergency.

There are a couple of tricks that can help you keep your balance. You can push against the water with your rod, getting the whole works in. You can also paddle a bit with your hands as a last resort.

Less than 6 inches of water over a greasy-slick stone bottom is probably the most dangerous situation you'll encounter, for a fall there can really hurt you. When the water's more than 2 feet deep it's a good cushion.

It's pretty obvious that you should be cautious about entering a swift stretch above a section that's over your head, but chest waders secured by a belt aren't the death traps they've been called. In a series of tests, wearing heavy waders, I was unable to fall or jump into water so that I couldn't keep my head up and swim slowly.

Inflated circular floats, which began with inner tubes, are very good for fishing lakes and slow-moving sloughs, although they can't be controlled in fast water. There are three types, one being a large inner tube with a canvas seat in the center, and the best of those have the tube completely contained in a zippered cover. Then there's the simple plastic "floater bubble," which has the same contours but is all plastic without the canvas. A third type is rigid polyethylene and generally has the most comfortable seat of all, but it takes up considerable space in transit.

These floats can be propelled in deep water without any sort of

Deep wading in swift water is no occupation for the faint of heart. This angler, John Bailey, is reaching for a distant bank.

fins if you simply kick yourself along backward. Regular swim fins give you added control and speed, and there are several types of fins made specially for the purpose, folding back as the feet move forward and pulling as they are moved back. For fishing in small areas these are more trouble than they're worth, for they're hard to walk in, but if you're going a long distance where you can't touch bottom they are well worthwhile. Small hand paddles such as those used for table tennis can be kept out of the way until needed.

These fisherman's floats are invaluable for some hike-in trips to small lakes. Inflated or rigid floats, however, are awkward loads on brushy trails.

BOATS

Many trout fishermen never have any occasion to fish from a boat, but then again, many do, and for them the use of boats requires attention. Of course, any safe craft from canoe to cruiser is usable on big natural lakes or impoundments. On rapidly moving rivers the choice is considerably narrowed, but boats become more and more important in gaining access to fishing water. Although laws are vague, it's generally possible to fish navigable streams without an adjoining landowner's permission, as long as the angler stays below the high-water mark in or out of the water. Thus, "float fishing" is the best and sometimes the only way of reaching some excellent water, even if not much fishing is done from the boat itself. A large percentage of the guided trout trips depend on boats, and there's no reason why a serious fisherman can't use his own.

You can divide river craft into two obvious classifications: those which must go faster than the current to maintain steerage and those which are held back against it. The canoe or kayak is generally propelled forward with paddles in fast water. If you stop driving a canoe forward you can't effectively steer it, so canoes aren't the best rigs to fish from on swift stretches. It's better to use them to get to logical spots for wading or standing on the bank. But one of the best things about a canoe is the ease with which it is carried atop a car or portaged to difficult launching spots.

For years the most popular swift-water fishing boat was the inflated life raft—a sort of elongated doughnut that could be rowed or paddled. When deflated, it will go into a station wagon or even a large car trunk. It is extremely safe, but it's hard to control in bad currents and it's strongly affected by wind. In recent years there have been some inflated boats of all sizes that have more rigid construction, often employing keels and taking outboard motors. They're much more expensive than the life raft, but can be handled better because of their true "boat" shape.

For guided white-water trips, extremely large rubber rafts are stiffened with exterior metal frames, and the rowlocks are attached to the framework. Another popular float design is the McKenzie boat, which looks much like a Banks dory as used for generations by commercial fishermen. It has flaring sides and high bow and stern so that it can be held with oars against fast water or waves. The aluminum "johnboat," a slender craft for use with or without motor and light enough for cartop transportation up to a 14-foot length, has become very popular for rivers of moderate speed.

Modified rubber raft is used for fishing stream with brushy banks which make much of it virtually impossible for waders.

These are general classes of boats, and there are all sorts of local modifications. The Au Sable boat, for example, is a sort of cross between the johnboat and canoe and often beautifully made. Now and then you'll see very old double-ended wooden boats that go well under the oars, and there are a few new ones. On some swift rivers the jet boat takes the place of ordinary outboards. It isn't economical of fuel, but it avoids the problems of an exposed propeller in rocky shallows.

Except for the canoe, most of these rigs are held back against the current with oars, thus "lowered gently" over moderate rapids, and they go slower than the current most of the time. You can do that well with a canoe if you install a rowing rig, but it's very difficult with paddles. Nothing is more localized than boat design, and the same kind of water is handled with different craft in different parts of the country.

The McKenzie boat is ideal for floating swift rivers. High stern will accept large waves when held against them. The oarsman is Tom Morgan of the Winston Rod Company. The caster is Dan Bailey.

There are exceptions to everything. For example, poling a canoe is standard procedure in some parts of Canada, and it's possible to go up surprisingly steep water once you have the knack, though only for modest distances. In drifting down over good fishing water, some fishermen use heavy log chains as drags to slow their progress in canoes or other light boats.

There's some question about powerboats on shallow trout rivers, and they've been accused of destroying spawning gravels. There's no doubt they can put the fish down, but no two situations are exactly alike.

PHOTOGRAPHY

For many anglers this subject really has nothing to do with trout fishing, for the image they carry away with them inside their heads is the only one they care about. For others, however, a photograph that can help refresh that image, or help convey it to someone else, is a delightful adjunct to a day's fishing, and as camera equipment becomes smaller and handier, more and more anglers seem to be taking Pete Hidy's advice to "carry a camera in your creel."

Having once toiled for a decade as a professional photographer, I learned the hard way that there are some special requirements for fishing pictures, even those kept only as mementos. Here are a few comments for those who feel pictures are an essential element in fishing; others can skip to the next chapter.

The first rule of fishing-trip photography is to have the camera along. Especially for the walking and wading angler this requires some advance planning—remembering that bulky equipment is likely to be left where it will do no good. I have many fishing friends who have spent considerable money for cameras specifically for their fishing expeditions and then invariably leave them in the car or at home.

So unless you are a serious photo hobbyist (in which case you won't need advice from me anyway), compactness is the number one requirement for fishing cameras. I believe the best choice for most fishermen is a compact, full-frame 35mm camera. The term "compact" is now used in the photo trade to describe cameras of roughly half the size of the "standard" single-lens-reflex 35 that

Three types of cameras of interest to fishermen. Left to right, a Nikon, full-sized 35mm reflex camera; compact Rollei with built-in exposure meter; Nikonos, built for underwater use and capable of surviving rough treatment.

takes interchangeable lenses. Most of the little ones cost less than $150, even with built-in exposure meters and excellent optics. An exception is the small Leica CL, which costs considerably more but will accept an interchangeable lens. However, this may be more camera than you need.

The "compact"-35 business was started some years back by Rollei, and its models are still good choices, although they have plenty of competition now. All of these little cameras can be carried handily in a fishing vest, and you can get waterproof plastic bags to fit them. (Remember, you will eventually fall in.)

The very tiny cameras that take photos smaller than the full-frame 35 might be satisfactory for you, but there are many instances when you'll be thankful for the larger format.

I should mention one camera of special classification, the Nikonos, for this model was built for underwater photography and can be washed under a faucet. It's a little heavier and bulkier than the "compacts," but requires very little care. However, it's also more expensive than most compacts and lacks a built-in exposure meter.

In general, keep the camera equipment simple and light—and take it with you.

One silly obstacle to good photo results is a strange psychological block against having a roll of film developed unless all of it has been exposed. If you have taken only a few frames and consider your pictures valuable, go ahead and have them developed; allowing film to molder in a camera is false economy. When you buy film, however, remember that the fat 36-exposure roll can be a curse to occasional photographers.

Pictures of fish work best when they are first caught. The fish, the enthusiasm and the locale are likely to deteriorate if you put off the picture taking. Yet strangely, picture time is often given grudgingly by the very people who will treasure photographs for a lifetime.

Since I buy groceries with my fish photographs, my friends may be a bit more tolerant of me, but when they get tired of posing it tends to show in the finished product.

Taking fishing pictures can be half the fun, although not every angler cares to be as burdened as the author is in this photo.

My pet approach is to say, "I'd like to set up some pictures. It'll take about fifteen minutes."

With that warning, my friends tend to relax a little, figuring they're in for it, and if I get the picture in 3 minutes instead of 15 they're pleasantly surprised.

If you read outdoor magazines and books you're sure to spot some obviously faked fishing action photos, but actually, a very large percentage of those which appear spontaneous are reenacted. The reason is that reenactment of a simple event can get you better pictures.

You say, "Pick the fish up out of the water again and this time turn to your right a little." A few months later the model has probably forgotten the treasured photo was a redo.

The most common fault of the rank amateur is to get too far back from his subject, but a little of this can help in fishing photography. Unless you are truly interested in a close-up of something, a little of the locale will help. The most successful fishing pictures I know of have included considerable scenery, with the actual fishing activity taking up only a small part of the frame. Incidentally, a fly line in the air amid appropriate scenery is often a very graceful shot. You don't always need a dead fish.

I have some old snapshots taken when I first began fishing as a youth, and although most of them show the fish I had caught, my interest now is more in the surroundings and the equipment. Thus I'd recommend that anytime you take a picture of a fish and fisherman, make a special effort to show the tackle.

And most of all, keep snapping away. Film is generally the cheapest element in the whole trip.

9 WHERE TO GO

I assume that you are going to start your trout fishing locally, and thus "where to go" will at first depend largely upon your own investigative prowess, acquaintance with other trout fishermen, possibly financial resources and other such considerations. However, if you're like most trout addicts, the time will come when you want to look beyond your local water—perhaps to find better fishing, but often to try a different kind.

Advanced anglers invariably develop preferences for certain approaches. Some become primarily interested in select fish that are especially hard to come by, some prefer big fish in big waters and some will go to no end of trouble or expense to find wilderness fish that are easy to catch, the trip itself being much of the fun. However, even the most sophisticated specialists usually enjoy a change of pace occasionally.

183

It is impossible to catalog all the various kinds of trout fishing entirely by geography, yet the various areas certainly do have more or less "typical" waters. Accordingly, in this chapter I'd like to give you a rough idea of what some of the major trout-fishing areas of our country have to offer and then end up with a look at some of the opportunities outside our borders.

Trout streams of the eastern part of the country tend to be smaller, and since the landscape is not so upended as in parts of the West, they are not so swift. Thus, "gentle eastern streams" is a common phrase. Eastern fish have a reputation for difficulty, not so much because of the stream type as because of heavy fishing pressure, and you'll hear that a successful eastern fisherman will do well anywhere he goes—as long as the rivers aren't too big. All of that is generality, because there are difficult and easy streams all over the world. Generally, there is easy fishing where hatchery fish are planted regularly, regardless of the address. Hard-pressured wild trout become hard to catch.

New England still has some hard-to-reach water for brook trout, although the brookies have been replaced by rainbow and brown trout in many areas, to the displeasure of natives. Probably some of the plantings were ill advised, but in other spots the water quality would no longer support the persnickety brookie. Landlocked salmon remain quarry in many lakes and streams of New England, especially Maine, and there's a beginning of a renewed Atlantic salmon run in Maine, but it will be some time before U.S. Atlantic salmon fishing will reach a stature to support many fishermen. There are lake trout in many New England ponds and lakes. Incidentally, "pond" in this region often means a large body of water that would automatically be called "lake" farther west or south.

New York has the best-known trout streams in America, partly because they have been easily accessible to fishermen from the large cities. Best-known of the names are the Beaverkill, Esopus, Neversink, Willowemoc and Delaware, and some of the world's best trout fishermen have developed there. Those rivers come down from the Catskills. The Adirondacks have others, and possibly the Ausable is best-known of those. These streams afford great variety, ranging from hatchery fish to highly technical targets. Access is generally easy on the well-known waters. On the smaller streams the crowds

Early-season view of the Beaverkill in New York.

can be escaped after the season's start. Late spring and early summer are the most reliable times. Fishing can get tough on warm late-summer water.

There is trout fishing all the way south to northern Georgia, and no one has sampled all of it. The Pennsylvania streams have become especially famous for their sophisticated fish and for well-established fly hatches, subjects of whole volumes of angling lore. The Letort and Yellow Breeches near Carlisle are among the best-known Pennsylvania names. The "limestone streams" of Pennsylvania have produced their own cult of fishermen and the Letort heads that list, with some of the world's most polished anglers visiting it. The fish are large and usually very difficult. The Letort, like many top waters, is fished only with flies, and only trophies over 20 inches may be kept. So although the Letort is very nearly a downtown stream, its restrictions and its difficulty usually save it from excessive crowding.

The Letort is an outstanding example of a unique stream. Although its water is extremely fertile—a handful of watercress there will appear to squirm with freshwater shrimp and sow bugs—the nature of the bottom is not conducive to extensive mayfly hatches. Therefore, there is an accent upon terrestrial-insect imitations more than upon water-bred types, and some of the "terrestrial" flies now used elsewhere were first tied for the Letort. It is limestone water, but hardly typical limestone water.

Wherever there are mountains in the eastern states there are trout streams, although most of the fishing depends heavily upon stocking. Southeastern waters cannot compete with streams of the West or North, but anyone willing to prospect and walk a bit might have some pleasant surprises. Years ago, I condescendingly hiked for miles up Hazel Creek, which empties into North Carolina's Fontana Reservoir, and found excellent fishing for "wild" trout, many generations removed from original plantings. More recently, I have found the North Carolina hills productive of a variety of trout fishing, even to stockers yanked out by casual fishermen using canned corn as bait.

The first rainbow I ever caught was a planter in Missouri, and the hilly parts of the southern Midwest still maintain a tenuous fishery for trout, largely hatchery fish. A unique kind of fishing is found

Wading "walkways" are used on the Letort in Pennsylvania near home of Charles K. Fox. Walkways save stream vegetation. Fisherman is William Downey.

Swift boulder and pocket water on the South Mills River in North Carolina. In this water there may be very few visible rises, and the caster must study every yard of current.

beneath some of the big dams in hill country where planted trout may grow huge but fail to reproduce. Nearly all of the power dams of that country were built across black bass streams, but the discharge from deep reservoirs is too cold for bass, at least for some miles downstream, and that's where the trout fishery comes in.

The midwestern Great Lakes states—Michigan, Wisconsin and Minnesota—have had their ups and downs in trout fishing, always maintaining it for the enthusiast, though at present the footloose trout man tends to go farther west. The famous trout rivers of that northern tier of the Midwest are apt to be crowded. The small streams that require a bit of walking are holding up well.

It is the Pacific transplants, especially the coho and the steelhead, which provide the most spectacular angling of the Great Lakes. The fly fisherman, spinner or plugger who wants to operate in shallow water generally competes with snaggers for the fish heading upriver to spawn. If he has the time, a fly fisherman using steelhead gear can watch river mouths and find striking cohos just as they begin their spawning runs—but the tourist fisherman isn't advised to try that unless he has a local source of information. The short-term visitor with no contacts will do better to troll from a charter boat.

The most extensive good trout fishing in the United States is found in the western states. Arizona and New Mexico are best-known for their backcountry streams, such as those in the vicinity of the Grand Canyon, but also afford good lake fishing, though this doesn't generally lend itself to fly casting.

Colorado has famous rivers of all sizes, but the best of that fishing is on the west side of the Continental Divide, mainly because of large population centers on the eastern slope. There's a great deal of stocking in Colorado. Some of the most famous rivers are the Frying Pan, Gunnison, North Platte, Taylor Fork and Roaring Fork. This is backpacking and horse-packing country, and Colorado's procession of very high mountains carries excellent tree-line lakes and cold-water creeks.

Wyoming is one of the leaders in trout fishing, some of the best being in the western part of the state. The Green River and North Platte are especially famous, but when you get to the Yellowstone National Park area you're in what's becoming the trout-fishing Mecca. Park management has been keyed to the serious trout fisherman lately, and there's top fishing all around the park as well as in it. Some of the best-known centers for fishermen are West Yellowstone at the west entrance to the park; Jackson, Wyoming, on the south and Livingston and Ennis, Montana, on the north.

Montana fishing has received a great deal of deserved publicity. At first it was largely devoted to the big "freestone" rivers such as the Missouri, Madison and Yellowstone, which arise in the Yellowstone Park area; but now a great many anglers are making pilgrimages to the "spring creeks" which flow for the most part over private ranchland. Fishing them requires permission these days, and frequently a fee. State fishing-access areas are usually on bigger water.

All of these Rocky Mountain states have high-country streams and lakes open to the public, but they've been taking a special beating lately through the boom in backpacking. A few years back most high-country anglers went by horse packtrain, but now hikers keep most of the trails dusty, and one longtime mountain fisherman told me his least-fished waters are often nearest the roads.

"It's nice for us old folks," he commented.

Good Western headquarters (for "areas" rather than individual streams) include Ketchum, Idaho; Saratoga, Lander and Pinedale, Wyoming; Glenwood Springs, Aspen and Durango, Colorado, and most western Montana towns.

Remember what I've said about high-altitude water conditions. In spring, many streams are running clear, simply because the mountain snows have not melted, but after that the torrents of melted snow water may keep some valley rivers muddy right up until July or August, depending upon how much snow fell in the mountains. Generally speaking, late summer and early fall are most reliable for the Rocky Mountain states.

Trout streams originating in lower country have a simpler pattern. In the eastern United States melting snows make the rivers high and muddy in spring, but only heavy rains produce that condition later on. Fall cold snaps accompanied by snow can cause water trouble farther north. For example, in British Columbia short rivers such as the famed Kispiox, where so many contest-winning steelhead are caught, can be especially tricky in early fall. The Kispiox is fed from low mountains, and when there's early snow followed by hot sun, unhappy fishermen watch their river turn chocolate. Short

A fisherman wades a real rushing torrent in the Rockies. In water like this, good-sized trout can survive in unseen shelters.

visits to such water are tricky, for the level goes up and down like a yo-yo.

The best California trout streams are mainly in fairly high country. Steelhead fishing in northern California, Oregon and Washington has done much to develop distance casters, for it's sometimes a sort of casting contest with fish as prizes. All of the Pacific coast states have trout fishing, but their rivers have suffered from damming. As fly casters have developed greater distance and have learned to use sinking lines and even lead-core shooting heads, they have begun to take their toll of other Pacific salmon as well as the coho, or silver, some of them caught considerably offshore. Frankly, the best small-stream trout fishing is found in the Rocky Mountain area, but there's some dramatic light-tackle big-water fishing along the Pacific, and it may be just beginning.

Alaska has become an expensive place to travel to, but there is exceptional Pacific salmon and steelhead fishing there. Anyone who wants to fish salmon should study the exact times to expect the runs. There are some spots where lake trout can be caught in shallow water shortly after ice-out and a few where they can be found shal-

Ultralight spinning gear used on small cohos (silver salmon) in Alaska stream. This fish, although still plump, was beginning to show signs of prespawning deterioration and was some distance from salt water.

low during the entire summer. Travelers of the Alaska Highway can find considerable good fishing of a wide variety if they take their time. The best fly fishing I've found near the highway to and within Alaska has been for grayling. A little inquiry will locate them, and for the most part they aren't overfished, Alaska visitors being interested mainly in bigger quarry. But to someone who has walked for miles to catch 6-inch grayling and returned them carefully, plenty of such fish more than a foot long is heady stuff on dry flies. Some of the Yukon Territory grayling fishing is especially good, as is that in Alaska, and I've spent some happy hours with grays in northern Alberta. The biggest grayling are in the Northwest Territories.

The Far North of both Alaska and Canada has the arctic char, a migratory spawner caught in great numbers in coastal rivers.

Where the silver salmon (coho) is concerned, the fish seem to behave differently almost everywhere they're caught, sometimes taking flies, but in some areas insisting on hardware or bait. Perhaps it depends upon the prespawning condition of the fish, but don't count on tearing them up with streamer flies unless you have advance information. I've taken some lumps in attempting that. In one Alaska creek I fly-fished for hours without a strike when a little spinner proved deadly.

Much of Canada has fine brook trout fishing of the wilderness variety. British Columbia is noted for truly big steelhead—fish that may be very large in comparatively small rivers. This fishing is reached both from the Pacific coast and by inland highway in some instances. Bush plane or helicopter is necessary elsewhere. The Skeena watershed has the Kispiox and Babine rivers, and other especially famous ones are the Fraser, Thompson, Dean and Sustut. Not much of the Northwest Territories can be reached by road, and charter flights are the rule for much of the arctic char fishing. There's good lake trout fishing in northern Saskatchewan lakes, and that too is largely fly-in country. Remote Quebec and Labrador have very large ouananiche—a form of landlocked salmon—as well as arctic char.

Eastern Canada is the most convenient destination for the Atlantic salmon fisherman from the United States. Newfoundland, with a great many short rivers, has the salmon in plenty, although it's not noted for the larger fish. The Labrador coast has excellent Atlantic salmon fishing, but for the most part it's not easily reached.

The most popular stomping ground for U.S. salmon seekers is New Brunswick, although much of its best water is privately owned or leased. The best-known New Brunswick river is the Miramichi. It gets plenty of fishing pressure, but success has improved since commercial fishing has been curbed by both Europeans and Americans.

Now let's briefly scan the fishing that exists farther afield, outside of North America, just to whet your appetite.

Atlantic salmon fishing in Iceland has become highly esteemed by American sportsmen. Some of the largest fish of all are hooked on plunging Norwegian rivers. And the salmon fishery of southern Europe, once considered lost, may now have a future. Salmon fishing in Britain also shows a likelihood of improvement, and the fish is

Atlantic salmon angler on Miramichi in New Brunswick beaches a grilse by simply walking backward as the fish tires, towing it to the shallows. The guide's net is not needed.

found as both sea-run and landlocked in other parts of the world. However, very few U.S. fishermen go specifically for salmon to foreign countries excepting Canada and Iceland.

By now, rainbow and brown trout are found almost everywhere in the world that conditions are acceptable to them. Two areas, southern South America and New Zealand, have attracted a great many Americans.

For a number of years, Argentina and Chile have called anglers seeking outsized trout, Argentina getting a head start which later faded a bit for political reasons. The Argentinean monsters are harder to come by these days because of increased fishing pressure, but they are still present. I get the impression that most anglers going there from the United States are primarily after big fish, a 10-pound brown sounding almost incredible to a fly fisherman who has been prizing 10-inchers all his life.

A good many of the largest fish are caught where rivers run into or out of the big natural lakes, many of the fish actually being lake residents which stage periodic feeding visits to river heads or mouths. So intent are most foreign visitors upon big fish that they pass up a great deal of other trout fishing, and some of the finest guides in the area know very little of the superb fishing for smaller trout to be had in lesser rivers of the Andes. Anglers insisting upon variety have found nearly virgin streams in rough country. As in North America, the largest fish of all are caught in lakes, usually by trolling or other deepwater methods.

The appeal of New Zealand, the other dream continent for U.S. fly fishermen, is somewhat different. Although there are many large stream fish there as well, they haven't quite matched the size of those in Argentina. But the dry fly and lighter tackle work better in New Zealand, and there are more and more package fishing tours sold by American promoters.

British trout fishing still attracts those looking for sophisticated waters, for the "chalk stream" (limestone) trout require a great deal of delicacy. Those waters are privately controlled, and such fishing is rather expensive even once you get there. However, part of the appeal is the historical role of streams such as the Test and the Itchen, both of which may be fished for a price, and both of which contain some fine fish.

The mainland of Europe still provides some of the finest trout fishing in the world, but there has been little promotion of it on this side of the Atlantic. The streams there are generally fished for a moderate daily fee. Most of the American casters are in Europe for other reasons in addition to their fishing. The same is true of South Africa.

Any good trout-fishing trip begins with homework. Most state tourist agencies or conservation agencies will provide general information, and probably maps, on the subject. Next comes the more detailed local steering, and city chambers of commerce can be a help, especially if guides are to be involved.

Finally, if you arrive on the scene with only vague plans, visit local tackle stores. There your reception depends largely on your approach, and buying something won't alienate the merchants. In fact, I have a policy of deliberately saving some fly purchases for the local dealers. If you have also studied the area enough to make a couple of intelligent queries, you'll be far ahead of the game. Whatever else, be sure you make it plain you are not a meat fisherman with a big icebox in your car. Somehow slip it into the conversation that you release most of your trout, if you do—and if you don't, you should.

10

GETTING IN DEEPER

Everything about trout fishing has been written, a good deal of it more than once, for it is the most literary sport of all. If he had the time and tackle, a reasonably literate beginner could retire to a good stream with an armful of books and become an expert without ever seeing or speaking to another angler.

But because there is so much written about trout by authors more engrossed in literary expression or highly advanced techniques than in basic fishing, some fishermen wade much deeper in print than they do in water. In no other endeavor is it so easy to skip fundamentals and plunge into fads, cults, hero worship and equipment collecting. Literary flights and advanced entomology are happy parts of the game but will be more appreciated if the new angler gets the basics first. The basics are what I've tried to give him in this book; and now I'll try to advise about more advanced reading— some of which is mainly for pleasure, some of which is mainly for information and all of which, hopefully, affords some of both. A more extensive sampling of fishing books with brief annotations appears at the end of the book in Appendix A.

You should be forewarned that many anglers in other fields think trout fishermen are funny-looking and funny-acting and that they take their literature too seriously. Until the modern bass fisherman came along with his brilliant jump suit covered with advertising patches and club insignia, the trout fisherman in his chest waders and unusual vest was the basic comic relief.

One of the world's most traveled and efficient anglers says that trout literature is a little absurd, that it wanders verbosely in unimportant areas and that it is read mainly by people who talk much about fishing and do very little of it. That's pretty sweeping, but it's indisputable that the literary technique of some treasured angling prose wouldn't be good enough to score in other fields.

I had a cultivated visitor some years ago who dazzled me with a profound knowledge of insects and tackle and had visited most of the prime trout spots of the world. I learned what I could from him, and after two hours of illuminating talk he confided to me that he had never learned elementary casting and wondered where he could get some instruction. He'd avoided the basics for years and was missing them more all the time.

Another extreme was one of the finest trout anglers I have ever known who used only one fly in several sizes, had no name for it and couldn't remember where he'd gotten the first one before he learned to tie reproductions. He had no interest in or knowledge of any trout water more than 2 hours' drive from his home. I hope you'll be somewhere between those extremes.

In discussing trout literature I'm going to begin with a little angling history—not that it necessarily comes first in importance, but we have to start somewhere, and the mention of some of the saints of the order is sure to come up now and then. You can learn the essentials about them in a few hours of reading, and if, your appetite thus whetted, you become a trout historian, collecting shelves of musty volumes on the subject, there's no harm done and it may be more fun than fishing.

It is quite possible, even likely, that fishing methods of other countries developed at about the same pace as or may have outdistanced those of Britain, but American trout fishing has, for the most part, an English history. Our students of the subject simply haven't unearthed much other literature, and early accounts have a way of getting around to Dame Juliana Berners and *A Treatyse of Fishing with an Angle,* which was part of a book printed in 1496. We're not even sure Dame Juliana, said to have been prioress of a nunnery, actually wrote the material, but it's pretty obvious that rather sophisticated fly fishing had been done long before that, because the *Treatyse* describes flies, horsehair leaders and rods. Moreover, the flies described in the *Treatyse* would be completely suitable for much of today's fishing. For that matter, there is a record of the Macedonians of about A.D. 200 using flies made of feathers.

Gaps in angling history are easily explained. Fishing, in early times, simply wasn't very important as a sport, and hunting, which had some of the elements of warfare, was preferred by the ruling classes. Long after the first angling books were written, sport fishermen were considered idlers, and strict American churchmen disapproved of the sport for more than two centuries.

Izaak Walton published *The Compleat Angler* in 1653, and in a later edition, 1676, Charles Cotton contributed a section on the more technical aspects of fishing. Walton was primarily a bait fisherman, and Cotton knew about flies. It wasn't so much Walton's angling knowledge that made him famous as his contemplative approach to it and to the joys of nature. Those earliest English writings were treasured by the few Americans who took fishing that seriously.

The only American trout available to the earliest settlers was the eastern brookie, and in virgin streams it was so gullible that English experts had a low opinion of it. Atlantic salmon were too plentiful for high regard as a sporting proposition, their range extending well down the Atlantic coast. They were to become scarce in the United States even before the Civil War.

When Washington Irving tried to capture some of the Izaak Walton spirit in a fishing trip in the early nineteenth century, he didn't like the wilderness aspect of American streams and felt a gentleman's angling could better be done in England, where "every roughness has been softened away from the landscape."

Americans didn't come up with anything new on the trout scene until well into the nineteenth century, and some historians will say that American sport fishing didn't really begin until about 1830. Just when true fly casting began, using the line as a casting weight, no one knows, and it must have been a gradual development. We do know that the Americans tended toward somewhat shorter and lighter fly rods than those of the English, especially for salmon fishing, but an American trout rod of the nineteenth century was still likely to be 10 or 12 feet long.

Only a dedicated student will go back to the first American writers on fishing, for such background certainly isn't going to be as helpful as later material. Accordingly, we'll look only briefly at a few of them and their contributions. You'll see them quoted from time to time, and their material is often stolen without credit. In fact, even back in Walton's day it was common to lift someone else's fishing material, and recent literary discoveries reveal that Izaak did it himself. The fishing writers were invariably fishermen themselves and became famous anglers because they were automatically self-promoted. This doesn't mean they were the best of their time, simply that they were the best-known; some of the world's best anglers today are unheard of outside a small circle of acquaintances.

Most early American sport angling went unrecorded, but it gained a voice in 1831 when New York's *Spirit of the Times* magazine began a fishing section of letters and articles that continued until the Civil War. The first professional angling editor on the American scene was Henry William Herbert, a displaced English aristocrat who wrote under the name of Frank Forester and published his first book, *Fish and Fishing*, in 1849. However, by then Dr. Jerome Smith, a fly fisherman for trout and landlocked salmon, had already published a "Practical Essay on Angling" as part of a book on the *Natural History of the Fishes of Massachusetts* in 1833, and John J. Brown, a New York tackle dealer, had written an American Angler's Guide in 1845.

The esthetic joys of fishing were extolled by Thaddeus Norris with *The American Angler's Book* in 1864, and his approach was similar to that of Walton. By that time, a few skilled trouters were using a "dry" fly. They weren't rigging it to float indefinitely, but by switching it dry between casts they could make it stay on top for a time, giving the trout a chance at a floater. Norris also described true fly casting, using the weight of the line to gain considerable distance, and discussed the disagreement (probably very old even at that time) between users of "attractor" flies and those believing in "strict imitation."

Charles Hallock, the founder of *Forest and Stream* magazine in 1873, wrote a number of books on angling, including one on fishing in Alaska. In the latter part of the century Dr. James S. Henshall became a leading authority on all forms of fishing and developed the "Henshall rod," which was intended for bait fishing but was built to duplicate the balance and feel of the better trout fly rods of the time.

Genio Scott wrote *Fishing in American Waters* (1869), Robert Roosevelt wrote *Superior Fishing* (1865), W. C. Prime specialized in entertaining stories with *I Go A-Fishing* (1873) and George Lawson wrote *Pleasures of Angling* (1876).

There was much talk of "scientific fishing" in those days, and light lines or leaders were considered a mark of skill. Long rods were considered more sporting than short rods, and much study was devoted to rod materials, some rods being made from several kinds of wood to establish desired action through their entire lengths. When split bambo appeared it was the beginning of lighter rods and truly controlled actions. The technique was first called "rent and glued," and "laminated" is probably the best description, but "split bamboo" will stay with us. Bamboo had been used for fishing rods for a long time before it was split and glued.

The split-bamboo probably appeared first in England, but the "invention" of the American split-bamboo rod by Samuel Phillippi of Easton, Pennsylvania, in the 1840s is a landmark. No matter whether it was borrowed from the English or not, by late in the century the American product was beating the British in casting competitions. From the first, the rent-and-glued rods seemed to have superior action. Eventually, the six-strip rod became most popular, although all sorts of combinations were tested. At first it was very difficult to make the strips stay together; thread wrappings were extremely important until after World War I when glues improved. Even the finest works of the old masters are known to separate under adverse conditions, for the old glues simply weren't waterproof.

You will hear a great deal about Theodore Gordon, the first leader in American dry-fiy fishing, and although he may not have invented a method, he certainly adapted one to American trout water, and he tied flies of his own to suit conditions in eastern America. Gordon was born to well-to-do parents in Pittsburgh in 1854, and after fishing other waters he retired, while a young man in ill health, as a semirecluse to live the rest of his life on the Neversink in New York's Catskills. He'd been fishing some flies upstream in primitive dry-fly fashion, but in 1890 he wrote to Frederic Halford, who was England's advocate of the dry fly, and after receiving samples of British imitations he tied flies of his own to match American conditions. He wrote on fly fishing in *Forest and Stream* and also served as American correspondent for England's *Fishing Gazette*. The Quill Gordon fly was his creation.

Gordon died in 1915, but it was some time later before his full fame was realized and his techniques became accepted by what has been called the "Gordon school" of trout fishing. Gordon came at an important time in American trout angling, for the rainbow trout had come east and the brown trout, introduced in America in the 1880s, had brought with it all the guile of its European ancestors. From then on the British had no reason to belittle the attractions of trout fishing in the United States.

After the century ended a disagreement arose about ethics which continued to be heard in England for generations and is still good for arguments. After the English had accepted the dry fly somewhere in the mid-1800s it became the gentleman's fishing method, and when the advanced nymph fishermen came along they were widely criticized. G. E. M. Skues, who wrote *Minor Tactics of the Chalk Stream* in 1910, advocated nymphs and wet flies when they seemed practical and became the outstanding exponent of underwater flies. The feud never reached so high a level in America. For one thing, only a fraction of the American waters were fished "to rising fish," whereas that was the established method on English streams and some anglers fished "only to the rise."

One other angler of the past deserves special attention: Edward Ringwood Hewitt (1866–1957). Born to a wealthy family, he became a student of angling techniques, fished over much of the world for trout and salmon and was a leader in ultralight tackle on salmon and the use of nymphs for trout. He showed excellent results with "skating" flies and was one of the first to use dry flies on Atlantic salmon. His written works are excellent texts today.

And now let's look at some of the more recent books written about trout and trout fishing. This is not a critique. The contents of most are pretty obvious from their titles, and others require a bit of explanation. A great deal has been written about trout, and this is intended as a representative sample rather than a selection. A somewhat more extensive listing will be found in Appendix A.

Before considering any other books you might take a look at one by Arnold Gingrich, founder of *Esquire* magazine, called *The Fishing in Print*. Mr. Gingrich was a devoted trout fisherman who seems to have shared the attitude of those who maintain that other forms of angling don't belong in literature; his book might well have been titled *The Trout Fishing in Print*, as there's not much in it about other kinds of angling. The book is a guided tour through the entire literature and is long on history, including perceptive comments on the works of the old writers, beginning with Dame Juliana.

So if you want a boildown of trout-fishing literature, Gingrich has it for you. His is in no way a how-to book, though in his closing pages he comes up with sound assessments of some recent books that are.

One of the good things about Gingrich's coverage is that he relates the development of angling to the literature as it appears. Gingrich was a literary man.

Before leaving the subject of trout books, I might mention that there is no law against someone who fly-fishes primarily for trout using the skills thus gained for angling with similar tools for other fishes from black bass to tarpon. Thus, you might want some general books on fly fishing—even the one I wrote myself called *Modern Fresh and Salt Water Fly Fishing*, which treats trout angling as just one of the fly-fishing games. (The public proved remarkably able to get along without that one, at least to start with, and the book is now out of print in hard cover. However, a fat paperback of it is available from Collier Books.)

Joe Brooks also did a general book, called *Fly Fishing*, back in 1958—a good, thorough coverage of the sport at the time, which has since been reissued. He also wrote a separate book on *Salt Water Fly Fishing* in 1950, the same title being used twenty years later by

George X. Sand. Sand's book is a compendium of history plus the opinions of a number of different practitioners. A good one-man job is Lefty Kreh's *Fly Fishing in Salt Water,* and another is A. D. Livingston's *Flyrodding for Bass.*

Among encyclopedic books covering all kinds of fishing, nothing surpasses the monumental *McClane's New Standard Fishing Encyclopedia,* a fine all-around reference library in one volume. Weighing in at several pounds, this one is pretty hefty and not cheap, but it's as close to being authoritative across the board as anything you'll find. At the other end of the scale fall the booklets issued by various manufacturers, such as the Cortland Line Company's "There's No Fishing Like Fly Rod Fishing." Some of these are surprisingly good, and most include handy diagrams of knots that are easily slipped into a pocket at the stage when you don't quite have them down by heart.

Trout fishing is also quite handsomely served by the periodical literature. The big three—*Field & Stream, Outdoor Life* and *Sports Afield*—run trout-fishing material quite steadily throughout the year, of course, but there are also three specialized magazines. *Fly Fisherman* (Manchester Village, Vermont 05254) is heavily weighted toward trout fishermen both editorially and in its advertising columns. *Trout,* the official publication of Trout Unlimited (P.O. Box 361, Denver, Colorado 80201) gives excellent coverage, and another top-notch publication is *The Flyfisher,* a quarterly published by the Federation of Fly Fishermen (519 Main Street, El Segundo, California 90245). These are both fine organizations to join, whether with a member club or as an individual.

TROUT BOOKS

Flies and Fly Tying

Art Flick's Master Fly-Tying Guide
Art Flick
Crown
  Well-known fly tiers and their favorite patterns, with methods.

Atlantic Salmon Flies & Fishing
Joseph D. Bates, Jr.
Stackpole
  Copious material on flies and fishing from many sources.

A Book of Trout Flies
Preston J. Jennings
Crown
  Respected work on matching insects with artificials.

Comparahatch
A. N. Caucci & Robert Nastasi
Cortland Line Company
  Covers the basics of matching flies to natural insects.

The Completest Fly Tier
Reuben R. Cross
Freshet Press
  Detailed manual of methods, patterns and materials.

Creative Fly Tying and Fly Fishing
Rex Gerlach
Winchester Press
  Well-illustrated coverage of method.

Dressing Flies for Fresh and Salt Water
Poul Jorgensen
Freshet Press
  Flies and their construction by a master of the game.

Fishing Flies and Fly Tying
William F. Blades
Stackpole
  An expert's analysis of the tying art.

The Fly-Tyer's Almanac
Edited by Dave Whitlock and Robert H. Boyle
Crown
  Expert information on fly construction and choice.

Fly-Tying Materials
Eric Leiser
Crown
  Materials, their sources and how to prepare them for use.

Gray's Sporting Journal
1330 Beacon St.
Brookline, Mass. 02146
　Published seven times yearly. Also produces an annual issue devoted to trout and salmon. Called a "class" periodical by critics, the *Journal* aims at literary outdoor coverage.

How to Tie Freshwater Flies
Kenneth Bay and Matthew M. Vinci-guerra
Winchester Press
　Tying methods of patterns gained from a variety of sources.

Modern Fly Dressings for the Practical Angler
Poul Jorgensen
Winchester Press
　Important flies and how to tie them.

Noll Guide to Trout Flies
H. J. Noll
Davis-Delaney-Arrow Inc.
　A paperback outline of tying techniques and patterns used by some professionals in teaching new operators.

Streamer Fly Tying and Fishing
Joseph D. Bates, Jr.
Stackpole Company
　Fine collection of streamer flies from a wide range of sources.

Tying and Fishing the Thunder Creek Series
Keith Fulsher
Freshet Press
　How-to regarding streamers.

Angling Techniques

The Art of Chalk Stream Fishing
C. F. Walker
Stackpole
　A British authority informs on some of the world's most technical trout angling.

The Art and Science of Fly Fishing
Lenox H. Dick
Winchester Press
　Sound how-to given in an entertaining manner.

The Art of Tying the Wet Fly and Fishing the Flymph
Jim Leisenring and Vernon Hidy
Crown
　Advanced methods and viewpoints concerning wet flies.

The Brook Trout and the Determined Angler
Charles Bradford
Freshet Press
　Small volume devoted to habits of the brookie and methods of fishing for it.

The Complete Book of Fly Fishing
Joe Brooks (revised)
Barnes
　A general work on fly fishing with considerable emphasis on trout.

Fishing the Midge
Ed Koch
Freshet Press
　A text devoted completely to fishing small flies for trout.

Fishing the Nymph
Jim Quick
The Ronald Press Co.
　Specialized material for both beginners and advanced anglers.

The Fly and the Fish
John Atherton (1951)
Freshet Press
> Techniques of fishing with a variety of fly types. Theory of color and texture in flies.

A Fly Fisher's Life
Charles Ritz
Crown
> The story of an ardent fisherman with some valid how-to information.

Fly-Fishing Heresies
Leonard M. Wright, Jr.
Winchester Press
> Techniques that break with tradition.

Fly Fishing the Lakes
Rex Gerlach
Winchester Press
> A rare approach, since most how-to trout books deal with streams.

Fly Fishing Strategy
Doug Swisher & Carl Richards
Crown
> Advanced techniques for difficult trout.

Fly Fishing for Trout
Richard W. Talleur
Winchester Press
> Well-written basic method for mature beginners.

Greased Line Fishing for Salmon
Jock Scott (Col. A. H. E. Wood)
Freshet Press
> An old work on Atlantic salmon techniques, some of them controversial.

Hatches
Al Caucci & Bob Nastasi
Freshet Press
> In-depth study of insects and their imitation.

How to Fish from Top to Bottom
Sid Gordon
Stackpole
> An all-around study of basic and advanced techniques.

How to Take Trout on Wet Flies and Nymphs
Ray Ovington
Freshet Press
> Subsurface fishing in detail.

The Lure and Lore of Trout Fishing
Alvin R. Grove, Jr.
Freshet Press
> First published in 1951, now with an updating preface. Entomology, fly tying and streamcraft.

Matching the Hatch
Ernest G. Schwiebert, Jr.
The Macmillan Company
> Sound and semitechnical story of insects, artificials and fishing methods.

McClane's New Standard Fishing Encyclopedia
Al McClane
Holt, Rinehart & Winston
> Nine pounds of fishing information, including much about trout and salmon.

A Modern Dry-Fly Code
Vincent Marinaro
Crown
> Opinionated fishing method with emphasis on limestone streams from an acknowledged master.

Modern Fresh & Salt Water Fly Fishing
Charles F. Waterman
Collier Books
What can I say? Some think this is pretty good, and there are plenty of copies left.

New Streamside Guide to Naturals and Their Imitations
Art Flick
Crown
Fine, brief treatise by a veteran in the observation and imitation of insects.

Night Fishing for Trout
James Bashline
Freshet Press
A seldom-covered subject about a time when many of the larger trout are on the move.

Nymphs
Ernest Schwiebert
Winchester Press
Extensive information on nymphs, how they live and how they are imitated with hair and feathers.

Nymphs and the Trout
Frank Sawyer
Crown
British river keeper and an outstanding nymph fisherman describes fishing in a variety of water.

The Philosophical Fisherman
Harold F. Blaisdell
Houghton-Mifflin Company
A general view by a veteran angler.

Rising Trout
Charles K. Fox
Foxcrest
Appealing angling information from one of the recognized authorities.

Selective Trout
Doug Swisher and Carl Richards
Crown
A how-to on fly selection.

The Soft-Hackled Fly
Sylvester Nemes
Chatham Press
Modern appraisal of wet flies and methods.

Steelhead
Mel Marshall
Winchester Press
A rundown on the seagoing rainbow.

Steelhead Paradise
John D. Fennelly
Mitchell Press (Vancouver)
Canadian steelhead rivers in review.

This Wonderful World of Trout
Charles J. Fox
Freshet Press
Angling techniques in pleasant prose.

Trout
Ray Bergman
Alfred A. Knopf
A classic and still valid work by one of America's most beloved authorities.

Trout Fishing
Joe Brooks
Harper & Row
One of the best books for complete coverage.

A Trout & Salmon Fisherman for Seventy-Five Years
E. R. Hewitt
Winchester Press
Fishing methods of one of the masters together with studies of fish behavior.

The Trout and the Stream
Charles Brooks
Crown
Ecology and tactics with emphasis on Western fishing.

Fish Studies

The Atlantic Salmon
Lee Wulff
A. S. Barnes & Co.
An old but thorough study of the fish and fishing methods.

The Compleat Brown Trout
Cecil E. Heacox
Winchester Press
A thoughtful study of the wisest of trouts and the methods of catching it.

Salmon of the Pacific Northwest
Anthony Netboy
Metropolitan (Portland, Ore.)
Hard-to-find rundown on salmon ecology.

Stream Conservation Handbook
J. Michael Migel
Crown
A treatise on stream management.

Through the Fish's Eye
Mark Sosin and John Clark
Harper & Row
One of the best descriptions of fish and how they operate.

Trout Streams
Paul R. Needham
Winchester Press
A reissued landmark work on the basic ecology of trout waters.

Mainly Entertainment

Coverts & Casts & Currents & Eddies (2 vols.)
William J. Schaldach
Freshet Press
Pleasant reading for atmosphere and sentiment.

Fisherman's Bounty
Nick Lyons, Editor
Crown
An entertaining anthology of fishing pieces.

Fishing Days, Angling Nights
Sparse Gray Hackle (Alfred W. Miller)
Crown
Entertainment with humor from one of the great trout-fishing veterans.

Fishing Widows
Nick Lyons
Crown
Humorous look at the angling fanatic.

A History of Fly Fishing for Trout
John Waller Hills
Freshet Press
Detailed coverage of the angling literature from the beginning.

The Last Pool—Upstream and Down and Big Stony
Howard Walden
Crown
Two entertaining books issued in one volume deep in the sentiment of angling.

The Pleasures of Fly Fishing
V. S. (Pete) Hidy
Winchester Press
The scenery and atmosphere of trout fishing, conveyed by fine photographs and selected quotations.

Quill Gordon
John McDonald
Alfred A. Knopf
Fly-fishing history with emphasis upon Theodore Gordon.

Remembrances of Rivers Past
Ernest Schwiebert
The MacMillan Co.
Colorful prose from great trout and salmon rivers of the world.

A River Never Sleeps
Return to the River
Fisherman's Spring
Fisherman's Summer
Fisherman's Fall
Fisherman's Winter
Roderick Haig-Brown
Crown
The Haig-Brown books are among the most respected works on fishing subjects. Although they stress the atmosphere and sentiment of angling they also give sound facts about trout and salmon.

The Secrets of Angling
John Dennys (1813)
Freshet Press
A collector's item that appears in verse.

Trout Magic, Trout Madness and Anatomy of a Fisherman
Robert Traver
Crown
A fine collection of entertaining pieces about trout fishing.

The Trout, the Whole Trout and Nothing but the Trout
John D. Shingleton and Phil Frank
Winchester Press
A small practical book combining humor and how-to.

The Well-Tempered Angler
Arnold Gingrich
Alfred A. Knopf
Pleasant commentary and extended excerpts with emphasis on trout literature.

Where the Pools Are Bright and Deep
Dana Lamb
Winchester Press
Intriguing collection of atmosphere pieces.

The Year of the Angler
Steve Raymond
Winchester Press
Evocative study of seasonal change by a veteran angler and angling editor.

APPENDIX B

SOURCES FOR TACKLE AND SUPPLIES

Listed below by geographical area are some of the best-known tackle shops and dealers specializing in fly-fishing equipment and, in some cases, fly-tying equipment as well. It is based on the recommendations of several wholesalers and other fishermen as well as my own experience, and though it undoubtedly omits many dealers who equally merit inclusion, at least it is a start.

You'll note that few large general sporting-goods stores are listed, and I am sticking pretty well to the specialists. If you were in New York or Chicago, for example, you could assume that Abercrombie & Fitch would have plenty of tackle and someone who understood it, but I haven't attempted to list all such outlets.

Note that the firms marked with an asterisk (*) publish extensive mail-order catalogs.

East

American Anglers
  710 Linden Street
  Bethlehem, PA 19018
Angler's Roost
  Room 301
  141 E. 44th St.
  New York, NY 10017
The Battenkill "Angler's Nook"
  Box 67A
  Shushan, NY 12873
*L. L. Bean
  Main St.
  Freeport, ME 04032

Barry Beck
  1336 Orange St.
  Berwick, PA 18603
The Bedford Sportsman
  Depot Plaza
  Bedford Hills, NY 10507
Beegle's Orvis Shop
  336 First St.
  Aspinwall
  Pittsburgh, PA 15215
Clapp & Treat, Inc.
  674 Farmington Ave.
  West Hartford, CT 06119

Carl Coleman Sporting Goods
4786 Ridge Rd. W.
Spencerport, NY 14559

S. J. Cooper & Son
609 E. Main St.
Plymouth, PA 18651

Cross Fork Tackle Shop
Box 261
Main St.
Cross Fork, PA 17729

Harry & Elsie Darbee
Livingston Manor, NY 12758

Dean's
1240 Paces Ferry Rd.
Atlanta, GA 30327

Fireside Angler, Inc.
P.O. Box 823
Melville, NY 11740

*The Fly Fisherman's Bookcase &
Tackle Service
Route 9A
Croton-On-Hudson, NY 10520

Flyfisher's Paradise
Box 448
Pike St.
Lemont, PA 16851

Forest County Sports Center
Elm St.
Tionesta, PA

Hackle & Tackle Co.
Central Square, NY 13036

Jack's Tackle
301–550 Bridge St.
Phoenixville, PA 19450

Joe's Tackle Shop
186 Main St.
Warehouse Point, CT 06088

Eric Leiser
Fly Fishing Supplies
Rt. 9A
Croton-On-Hudson, NY 10520

*H. L. Leonard Rod Company
25 Cottage St.
Midland Park, NJ 07432

Markle's Sporting Goods
719 Grant St.
Indiana, PA 15701

Nemacolin Trail Hunting Reserve
Route 40, Box 67
Farmington, PA 15437

Oliver's Orvis Shop
44 Main St.
Clinton, NJ 08809

*The Orvis Company
Manchester, VT 05254

The Orvis Shop
5655 Main St.
Williamsville, NY 14221

Orvis Shop of Boston, Inc.
213 W. Plain St.
Wayland, MA 01778

The Plumlea Angler
Jackson Rd.
Fletcher, NC 28732

Rangeley Region Sports Shop
28 Main St.
Rangeley, ME 04970

The Rod & Reel
P.O. Box 132
Leola, PA 17540

Stoddard's
50 Temple Place
Boston, MA 02111

Dick Surette Fly Fishing Shop
P.O. Box 200
North Conway, NH 03860

Van Doren's Orvis Shoppe
Box 368
1007 Sycamore Sq.
Midlothian, VA 23113

Yellow Breeches Fly Shop
Box 205
Allenberry Rd.
Boiling Springs, PA 17007

Central

*Angler's Mail
  6497 Pearl Rd.
  Cleveland, OH 44130

Fred's Southern Flyfishing Shop
  117 W. Main
  Decatur, TX 76234

Gates AuSable Lodge, Inc.
  Box 2828
  R.R. 2
  Grayling, MI 49738

*Herter's
  Waseca, MN 56093

Main Stream Fly Fishing Outfitters
  28956 Orchard Lake Road
  Farmington Hills, MI 48024

Orvis Shop of Arkansas
  7710 Cantrell Rd.
  Little Rock, AR 72207

Rockwell Springs Trout Club
  Box 305
  Castalia, OH 44824

Thornapple Orvis Shop
  Thornapple Village
  Ada, MI 49301

West

*Dan Bailey's Fly Shop
  209 West Park St., Box 1019
  Livingston, MT 59047

Pat Barnes Tackle Shop
  West Yellowstone, MT 59758

Bodmer's Fly Shop
  2400 Naegele Rd.
  Colorado Springs, CO 80904

*Buz's
  805 West Tulare Ave.
  Visalia, CA 93277

Creative Sports Enterprises
  2333 Blvd. Circle
  Walnut Creek, CA 94595

Jack Dennis Outdoor Shop
  Box 286
  136 Broadway
  Jackson, WY 83001

The Flyfisher
  315 Columbine St.
  Denver, CO 80206

Ned Gray Enterprises
  Box 373
  2615 Honolulu Ave.
  Montrose, CA 91020

*Kaufmann's Streamborn Flies
  12963 S.W. Pacific Highway 99W
  Portland, OR 97223

Norman S. Leighty, Inc.
  1033 Walnut St.
  Boulder, CO 80302

*Bud Lilly's Trout Shop
  Box 387
  West Yellowstone, MT 59758

The Mill Pond, Inc.
  59 N. Santa Cruz Ave.
  Los Gatos, CA 95030

Parks' Fly Shop
  Gardiner, MT 59030

Jim Poor's Anglers All, Ltd.
  5211 South Santa Fe Drive
  Littleton, CO 80120

Hank Roberts
  1636 Pearl St.
  Boulder, CO 80302

Streamside Anglers
  P.O. Box 2158
  Missoula, MT 59801

Will's Fly Fishing Center
  Ashton, ID 83420

R. L. Winston Rod Co.
  475 Third St.
  San Francisco, CA 94107

INDEX